SJP
SM

OP 18⁰⁰

D0218091

X
2.50

Pacific Gateway

An Illustrated History of the Port of Oakland

Woodruff Minor

design: Terry Lim

PORT OF OAKLAND

Copyright © 2000 Port of Oakland

All rights reserved under Universal Copyright Convention and Pan-American Copyright Convention.

Reproduction or translation of any part of this work beyond that permitted by Sections 107 or 108 of the 1976 United States Copyright Act without permission of the copyright owner is unlawful. Requests for permission or futher information should be addressed to:

Communications Division
Port of Oakland
530 Water Street
Oakland, CA 94607 USA
http:\\www.portofoakland.com

ISBN: 0-9678617-0-5

Library of Congress Card Number: 00-102306

Printed by Montague & Spragens, Inc. 196
Oakland, California

COVER ILLUSTRATIONS. *Left panel: Oakland Long Wharf as seen from Yerba Buena Island, 1880s. Center panel: Oakland International Airport, Terminal 1, 1960s. Right panel: Outer Harbor container cranes, 1980s. The airplane inserts are a Boeing 40, Pacific Air Transport, 1920s (left), and a Boeing 720, Southwest Airlines, 1980s (right). The photographs are from the Port of Oakland Archives.*

CONTENTS

For Sharon

FOREWORD

You are about to embark on a wonderful journey. This book is an account of the development of a national and local treasure—the Port of Oakland. The Port, known to many today by its harbor, airport, and commercial real estate, has been shaping the life and economy of the San Francisco Bay Area for seven decades. Oakland's evolution as a great harbor and transportation center has much earlier origins.

In the pages that follow, many intriguing questions are asked: How did Oakland become the designated terminus of the transcontinental rail system? When was the Port of Oakland established? Who manages the Port? Why did an airport develop near San Leandro Bay? What contributions did Oakland make to early aviation? Where is the Port of Oakland headed? The answers to these and other questions provide a picture of how this organization developed, who its main actors were, what the struggles were, and how the Port's relationship to the city of Oakland and its citizens developed.

Today, the Port of Oakland stands at an important juncture in its history. The Port's seaport will double in size, Oakland International Airport is poised for expansion, and the waterfront has emerged as a public asset to use and enjoy. It is fitting, then, that we examine our past to gain an understanding of how to move into the future.

This book endeavors to illumine a piece of Oakland's heritage that has become somewhat invisible. Many of the historic images gathered herein have been culled from old boxes and dusty files, and are brought together in this beautifully crafted volume to provide a visual dimension to the Port and its place in the history of Oakland. It is a very engaging and enlightening story that will undoubtedly engender a sense of pride in Oakland as a great California place.

We express our gratitude to everyone who participated in the preparation of *Pacific Gateway*. To those who contributed archival materials, to those who brought the value of our historical resources to our attention, and to those who are "active bearers" of Port history, we convey our heartfelt thanks. History is something we all carry with us. Sometimes it takes a project like this to help us appreciate the value of our own experience. Perhaps our efforts can serve as a model, to be used by other community groups or agencies to explore their own histories.

May strong winds fill your sails as you journey into the rich and textured history of the Port of Oakland.

Charles W. Foster
Executive Director

John Loh
President, Board of Port Commissioners

AUTHOR'S PREFACE & ACKNOWLEDGMENTS

The year 2000, which commemorates 150 years of California statehood, also marks the seventy-fifth anniversary of the Port of Oakland. On November 10, 1925, Oakland voters overwhelmingly approved bonds to expand the city's port facilities. Two months later, on December 11, Mayor Davie appointed five Oakland residents to a temporary board that would oversee the new port. The Board of Port Commissioners achieved permanence on February 12, 1927, following the passage of a charter amendment formally establishing the Port of Oakland. As a self-supporting, autonomous branch of the municipal government, the Port of Oakland has jurisdiction over the city's waterfront. With the exception of two bond issues for which the city has been reimbursed, the Port generates its own revenues through its maritime, aviation, and real-estate operations.

The Port of Oakland has enjoyed considerable success as a provider of maritime and aviation services. One of the nation's leading ports, Oakland links the Bay Area to a global intermodal system. Because of the Port, the region remains a major conduit of goods in the world economy as well as a player in the ongoing drama of transportation technology. At the same time, the Port as an institution has become increasingly responsive to the community and the environment. The Port of Oakland enters the twenty-first century with an increasingly sophisticated sense of its complex role as a public agency.

It is important at the outset to say what this book is *not*. It is not a social history, nor is it a history of technology or labor or local politics, though it touches on all of these things. Rather, it is the history of a public agency in the context of a city and a region. The book is divided into three sections, corresponding to the Port's three revenue-producing divisions—maritime, aviation, and commercial real estate. My goal has been to provide the reader with enough context and background to impart perspective and meaning to the institutional history. It is my hope that others may be inspired to delve more deeply into issues that I have only touched upon.

Chapters 1 through 4 trace the evolution of maritime activity in Oakland, beginning with its nineteenth-century origins as a city dominated by one railroad, which literally owned the waterfront. The early decades of the twentieth century brought rapid growth and a progressive government that succeeded in regaining control of the waterfront, leading to the establishment of the Port of Oakland, eventually one of the world's largest container ports. Chapters 5 through 7 cover local aviation history, from the balloon ascensions of the Gold Rush to the establishment of Oakland Municipal Airport and its transformation into Oakland International Airport. Chapter 8 provides an overview of the Port's real-estate developments, including Jack London Square and the Oakland Airport Business Park. Chapter 9 concludes the book with a discussion of the Port's relationship to the community, including issues relating to public access and environmental quality.

I wish to thank the Oakland Board of Port Commissioners and the Port of Oakland Maritime Division for funding this project. The book originated as partial mitigation for the 1995 demolition of a remnant of the Grove Street Pier transit shed at the Charles P. Howard Container Terminal. Helaine Kaplan Prentice, representing the Oakland Landmarks Preservation Advisory Board, and Betty Marvin, on the staff of the Oakland Cultural Heritage Survey, suggested the idea. The Port of Oakland Environmental Planning Department provided oversight. Special thanks to Dean Luckhart for shepherding the project into reality in 1996, and to Celia McCarthy for taking over management duties in 1998; their guidance and patience have been greatly appreciated. James McGrath, Loretta Meyer, and Richard Sinkoff also provided managerial support. Other members of the Environmental Planning Department who helped me along the way are Trish Anderson, Jon Amdur, Vickie Arnold, consultant Gayle Borchard, Ramona Dixon, Lauren Eisele, Maureen Gaffney, Kelley LeBlanc, Janet Meth, Kate Nichol, Delphine Prevost, Misi Pulu, Stefan Seum, Gail Staba, and Jody Zaitlin.

Many other Port of Oakland employees gave of their time, including David Adams, David Alexander, Michael Beritzhoff, Larry Berlin, Estrellita Boggess, Raymond Boyle, Roberta Bradley, Thomas Clark, Steven Clough, Vaughn Filmore, Robert Gardner, John Glover, Steven Gregory, Steven Grossman, Steven Hanson, Barbara Hawkins, Dennis Jackson, Harold Joseph, John Kaehms, Jack Knecht, Jim McIlvaine, Kristi McKenney, Joe Marsh, Christopher Marshall, Imelda Osantowski, John Prall, Jim Putz, Gerald Serventi, Terry Smalley, Jon Stark, Barbara Szudy, George Turner, Carole Wedl, Neil Werner, Dan Westerlin, Richard Wiederhorn, and Anne Whittington. Celia McCarthy gathered information for the shipping and revenue charts and historical maps. Assistant Art Director Ross Turner, who produced the appendix maps and shipping chart, spent additional hours tracking down images and taking photographs. Raymond Boyle, Michael Beritzhoff, and Ray King saw to the book's publication.

Thanks to my wife, Sharon, for her constant support (and editor's eye); to Michael Corbett, who helped me navigate the early chapters; to Betty Marvin, William Sturm, William Kostura, and Judy Millar for research assistance; and to Gary Knecht and Sandra Threlfall for sharing their knowledge of waterfront issues. For help in procuring photographs, I wish to thank Deborah Cooper, Marcia Eymann, and Diane Curry of the Oakland Museum of California; William Sturm of the Oakland History Room, Oakland Public Library; Analee Allen of the *Oakland Tribune*; Don Hausler of the Emeryville Historical Society; and Maxine Terner of the East Bay Regional Park District. Finally, my thanks to the copy editor, Vitalee Giammalvo, and to the indexer, Frances Bowles, for their fine work, and to Terry Lim for designing the book with such self-evident artistry.

Woodruff Minor
Berkeley, California

Maritime

Prior to 1910, Oakland's city-owned port facilities consisted of two small wharves and sheds adjoining the Webster Street Bridge. In this turn-of-the-century view, a stern-wheel steamer is berthed at City Wharf No. 2. To the left is City Wharf No. 1. The James P. Taylor coal yard (in background) was one of the largest on the estuary. (Courtesy of the Oakland History Room, Oakland Public Library.)

akland, the principal port on San Francisco Bay, plays an important role as a regional transfer point for goods carried by land and sea. The giant cranes of the waterfront and the constant comings and goings of ships, trains, and trucks attest to the port's prominence. Yet this maritime activity is only the most recent chapter in a long and distinguished history.

Introduction

Oakland's stature as a port is due to its location on San Francisco Bay. Covering hundreds of square miles, the bay is a great natural harbor containing the largest expanse of sheltered water on the Pacific Coast. Its two main tributaries flow through California's Central Valley. Over the years, this extended bay and river system has served dual functions as a moorage for oceangoing vessels and as the only water route to the state's interior.

San Francisco Bay has been an important working harbor since the Gold Rush, which transformed San Francisco into a major port. During the nineteenth century, the bay developed rich maritime traditions. Clipper ships carried passengers and cargo around Cape Horn. Sturdy vessels from the shipyards of Maine delivered manufactured goods. British barks brought coal from Newcastle, returning to Liverpool with grain. Lumber, salmon, and sugar flowed in through the Golden Gate.

Oakland was one of many small settlements that sprang up during the Gold Rush. Unlike other bayshore towns, the waterfront was owned by a single person who controlled all port development. In 1869, Oakland became the terminus of the transcontinental railroad and the state's most important rail center. Control of the shoreline then passed to the railroad, which monopolized local shipping for decades. At the same time, federal harbor improvements made the waterfront more accessible to oceangoing vessels, laying the foundation for the city's maritime development.

San Francisco during the Gold Rush. This 1851 view looks east over the crowded harbor to Yerba Buena Island. (Courtesy of the San Francisco Maritime National Historical Park.)

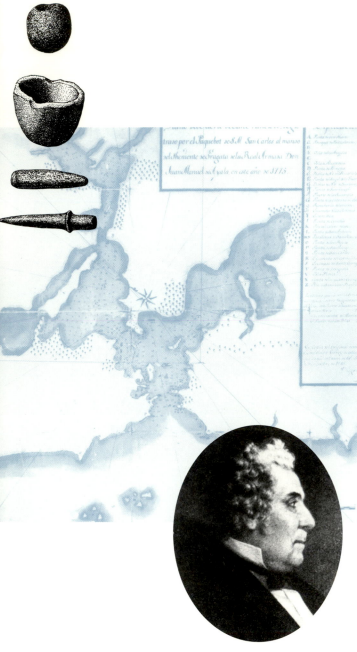

Vicente Peralta

Beginnings

Oakland did not exist as a town or city prior to the Gold Rush—it was first settled in 1850, the year California achieved statehood. Yet the site has a history of human settlement extending back centuries. The lush natural setting, containing forests of oak and redwood and a shoreline bordered by marsh and tideland, was replete with mammals, birds, fish, and crustaceans. Native Americans known as the Ohlone came into this area at least 1,500 years ago. They were hunters and gatherers who left little physical trace on the land except for shell mounds. At the time of contact with Europeans, the Ohlone inhabited much of the region between San Francisco Bay and the Carmel River.

In the eighty years prior to statehood, California was an outpost of the Spanish Empire and a province of Mexico. San Francisco Bay served as one of the colony's principal harbors and population centers. The bay was initially sighted in 1769 by a Spanish land expedition, and a Spanish supply ship entered its waters in 1775. The first colonists—settlers, soldiers, and priests—arrived in the summer of 1776. By the 1820s, the region had several hundred Spanish-speaking residents, concentrated in a military fort, a civilian town, and five missions where Native Americans were converted to Christianity and assimilated into the new agricultural economy.

Under Mexican rule, the Spanish missions gave way to private ranchos which carried on an extensive foreign trade in hides and tallow. This marked the true beginning of maritime commerce on San Francisco Bay. Cattle formed the basis of the colonial economy, especially during the heyday of the ranchos in the 1830s and 1840s. American and British vessels imported manufactured goods, returning around Cape Horn with hides for shoe and saddle factories and tallow for the production of soap and candles.

The Oakland area, known as the *contra costa* (Spanish for "opposite shore"), lay within the boundaries of Rancho San Antonio. Granted in 1820 to Luis Maria Peralta, who divided it among his four sons in 1842, this 45,000-acre estate was one the earliest and largest ranchos on San Francisco Bay. Along with Oakland, the property took in the sites of present-day Alameda, Albany, Berkeley, Piedmont,

2

Emeryville, and a portion of San Leandro. The Peraltas maintained embarcaderos, or landings, for shipping out hides and tallow across the bay. The main landing (Embarcadero de San Antonio) jutted into the estuary near the foot of today's Fourteenth Avenue in East Oakland.

During the rancho era, the most important moorage for foreign vessels was a sheltered cove on the west side of the bay, not far from the original presidio and mission. The town of Yerba Buena—later renamed San Francisco—was established there in the 1830s to serve as a regional center for the hide and tallow trade. It was to Yerba Buena Cove that the Peraltas and other rancheros shipped their goods by small craft. This village, soon to become a great city, would remain the major port on San Francisco Bay for over a century.

The Gold Rush and American Settlement

At the close of the Mexican War in 1848, California was ceded to the United States under the terms of the Treaty of Guadalupe Hidalgo. As the treaty was being signed, gold was discovered in the foothills of the Sierra Nevada. The ensuing Gold Rush, which precipitated statehood in 1850, set the stage for widespread settlement of the bay region, ushering in a new maritime era.

As the principal port of entry, San Francisco was suddenly transformed from a town of several hundred residents into a city of 50,000 inhabitants. Where once a dozen vessels might call over the course of a year, now there were hundreds. The city's rise as a port was sustained by merchants and private investors who built the first permanent wharves and warehouses.

San Francisco Bay and its tributaries were the lifelines of the new Gold Rush towns. To some degree, all towns were linked by water to San Francisco. Steamboats plied the rivers to the gold-field portals of Stockton and Sacramento. Scows and steamers sailed to numerous landings around the bay, such as Oakland, Alameda, Alviso, Redwood City, Petaluma, and Napa. San Francisco supplied the towns with people, capital, and imported goods; the towns provisioned the metropolis with lumber, firewood, fruits, vegetables, meat, and grain.

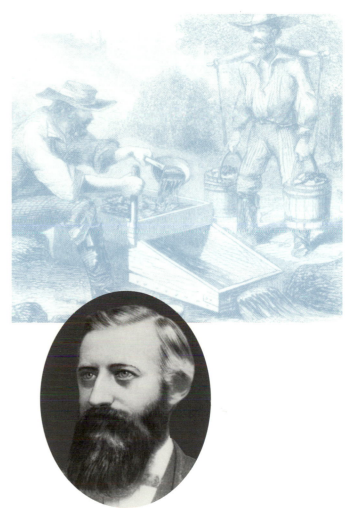

Horace W. Carpentier

Except for its bayshore location opposite San Francisco, there was little at first to distinguish Oakland from other Gold Rush settlements. In 1850, attorney Horace W. Carpentier and two associates laid claim to the original townsite, an expanse of Peralta land lying west of today's Lake Merritt. An act to incorporate the town was later secured in the state legislature. Passenger ferries and shallow-draft sailing vessels called at three small wharves at the foot of Broadway, Webster Street, and Washington Street, but the waterfront remained virtually undeveloped. Other wharves were located at the old embarcadero in the thriving lumber town of San Antonio (later Brooklyn), which shipped out redwood from the rapidly depleted forest in the Oakland hills. Clark's and Damon's Landings, both situated on the north shore of San Leandro Bay, served local farms and hamlets.

The Oakland *was placed in service by the Central Pacific in 1875. Twice rebuilt, this ferryboat carried transbay commuters for over sixty years. (Courtesy of the Oakland History Room, Oakland Public Library.)*

The 1852 act incorporating Oakland authorized the town trustees to build and maintain bridges, ferries, wharves, docks, and piers. State-owned submerged lands ("lying between high tide and ship channel") were granted to the town. At their first meeting, the trustees passed an ordinance "for the disposal of the waterfront belonging to the town of Oakland, and to provide for the construction of wharves." The recipient, Horace Carpentier, was given the exclusive right to operate port facilities. He agreed to pay the town five dollars, erect a public schoolhouse, build three wharves, and give 2 percent of the annual dockage fees. He was then granted ownership of the Oakland waterfront "forever." In 1854, Carpentier was instrumental in having the town reincorporated as a city, and he became its first mayor.

Carpentier also secured the ferry franchise. His company provided the first reliable ferry service on the bay, with regular crossings between Oakland and San Francisco. A rival estuary line, serving San Antonio and Alameda, soon merged with the Oakland line. By 1860, Carpentier controlled every aspect of the city's waterfront, from land titles to transportation.

The Railroad Era

Railroads brought fundamental change to California. Rail lines fostered urbanization, opened up the interior for development, and profoundly altered shipping methods. As California's principal rail terminus, Oakland benefited greatly from these changes. Yet the railroad also held the waterfront monopoly, thus inhibiting the city's port development.

The small local lines built in Oakland and Alameda during the Civil War were among the first in California. The San Francisco and Oakland Railroad began service in 1863, followed in 1864 by the San Francisco and Alameda Railroad. Both lines maintained deep-water piers on the bay, with frequent ferry crossings to and from San Francisco. These pioneer railroads were soon absorbed by the Central Pacific (CP), then in the process of building the western half of the transcontinental railroad.

Oakland's existing rail facilities and mainland site opposite San Francisco made the town attractive to the Central Pacific as a terminus. In 1868, the railroad entered into a partnership with Carpentier, resulting in the formation of the Oakland Waterfront Company. All land previously deeded to Carpentier was transferred to the new company, which granted rights-of-way for tracks and substantial acreage for yards and terminals. Despite repeated protests and lawsuits, the Central Pacific, reorganized in 1885 as the Southern Pacific (SP), sustained the monopoly for four decades.

The Oakland Long Wharf and Mole as seen from Yerba Buena Island in the 1880s. Square-riggers are clustered at the end of the wharf. To the right, closer to shore, is the passenger ferry depot. (Courtesy of the Oakland History Room, Oakland Public Library.)

The Oakland Long Wharf at the turn of the century, looking west to Yerba Buena Island. Deep-water sailing ships prepare to take on cargo from rail cars. (Courtesy of the Oakland History Room, Oakland Public Library.)

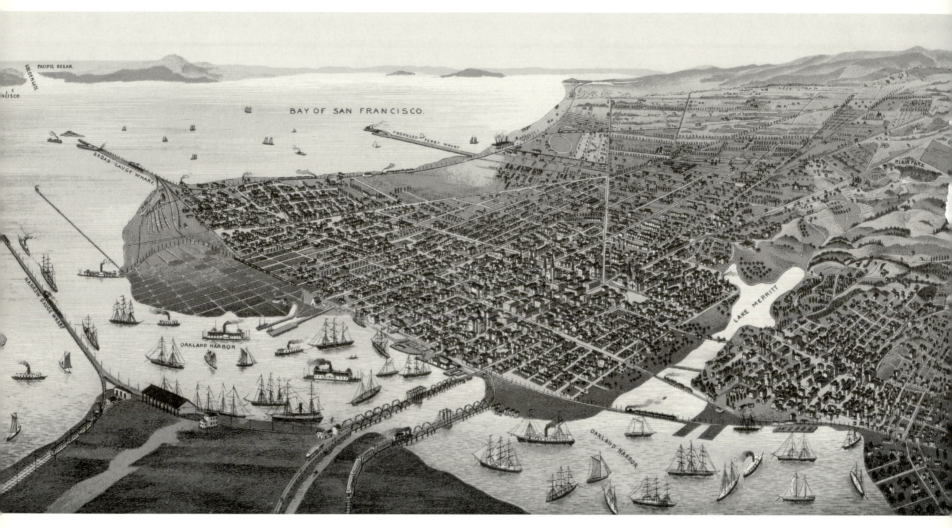

Bird's-eye lithograph of Oakland, 1893. Bridges at Webster Street and Alice Street span the estuary, identified here as "Oakland Harbor." (Courtesy of the Oakland History Room, Oakland Public Library.)

Transcontinental train service commenced late in 1869. Early in 1871, the Central Pacific completed its new freight and ferry pier on the western waterfront. Extending two miles into the bay off the end of Seventh Street, the Oakland Long Wharf was the single most important shipping terminal on the Pacific Coast. It incorporated train tracks, slips for passenger and freight ferries, and berths for deep-water vessels. The Oakland Mole, an earth-fill causeway for passenger trains and ferries, extended along the south side of the wharf. After the mole opened in 1882, the Oakland Long Wharf was used exclusively for freight operations.

By providing jobs and excellent ferry service, the railroad stimulated rapid growth in Oakland, which soon overtook Sacramento as the state's second largest city (a ranking it held through the turn of the century). During the 1870s, the population tripled to nearly 35,000; by 1900, it had increased to 67,000, about a fifth the size of San Francisco. Annexations in the 1870s and 1890s pushed the city's boundaries east of Lake Merritt to encompass the town of Brooklyn and north to the Berkeley border. Oakland's burgeoning downtown, centered around Broadway, was linked to outlying districts by streetcar lines. Bridges at Webster Street (1871) and Alice Street (1873) crossed the estuary to Alameda. Both cities prospered as commuter suburbs of San Francisco, with the ferries of the Central Pacific and Southern Pacific carrying millions of passengers annually.

During this same period, San Francisco consolidated its position as the region's leading port. In 1863, the state legislature passed a bill establishing the Board of State Harbor Commissioners, vesting it with power to build and regulate public wharves on San Francisco's waterfront. Over the next half-century, the commissioners would construct a six-mile-long seawall, numerous piers, a belt-line railroad, and a monumental ferry terminal. The Central Pacific and Southern Pacific accepted San Francisco's primacy as a port, and it became standard practice for goods to be transshipped across the bay to and from the Oakland rail terminus.

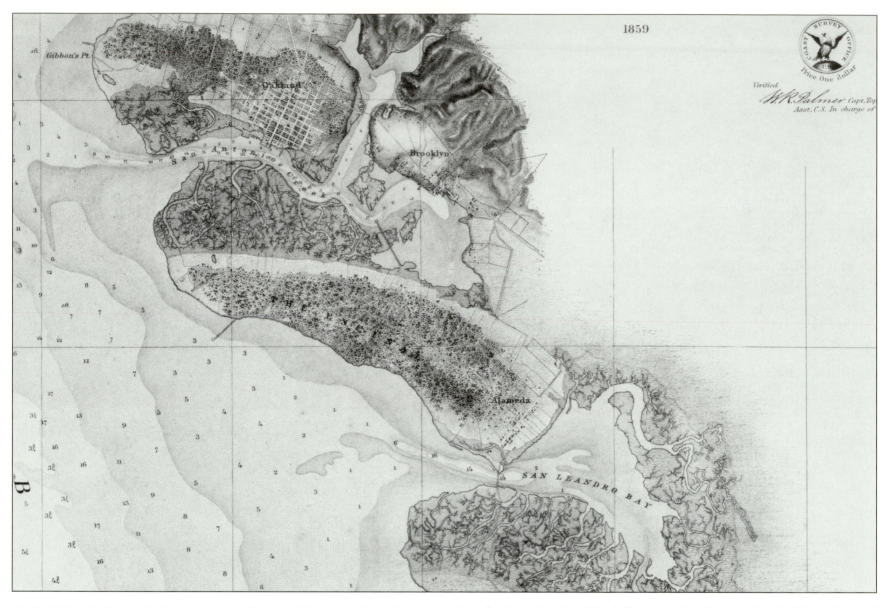

In the 1850s, Oakland and Alameda were small towns with a combined population of 2,000. Marsh and tideland bordered the shores. San Antonio Creek (now known as the estuary) meandered between Oakland and Alameda, terminating in shallow basins on the north (Lake Merritt) and east (Brooklyn Basin). The marshy peninsula south of San Leandro Bay is Bay Farm Island. (Entrance to San Francisco Bay, California: Survey of the Coast of the United States, U.S. Coast Survey Office, 1859. Courtesy of the Map Room, Doe Library, University of California, Berkeley.)

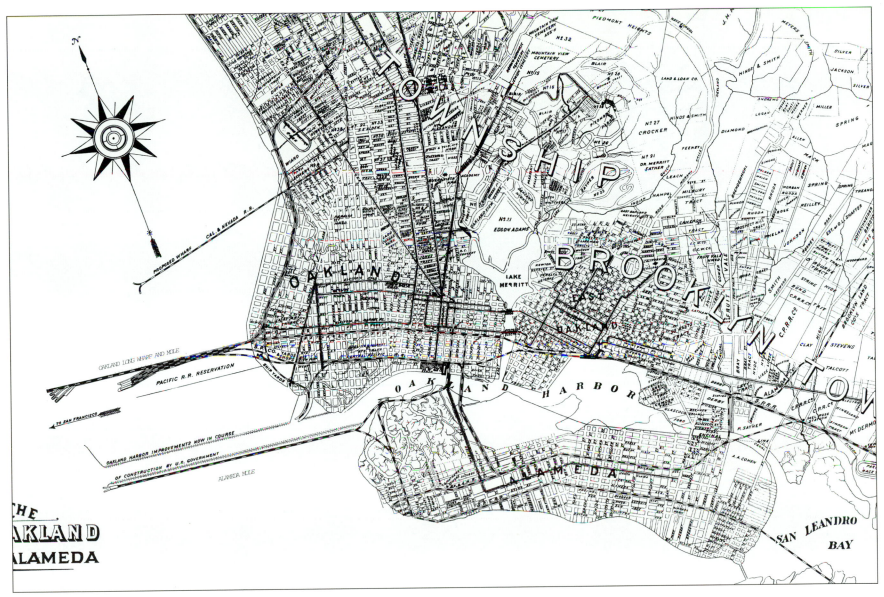

By 1900, railroads and transbay ferries had contributed to explosive growth in the East Bay, transforming Oakland and Alameda into thriving cities, with a combined population of 82,500. The oak forest has been supplanted by street grids, and there has been extensive reclamation of marshland. The Alameda Mole and the Oakland Long Wharf and Mole extend into the bay. Federal harbor improvements to the estuary (here labeled "Oakland Harbor") are evident in the training walls, reconfigured shoreline, and tidal canal. (Map of the Cities of Oakland, Berkeley and Alameda: George F. Cram, Chicago, 1901. Courtesy of the Map Room, Doe Library, University of California, Berkeley.)

View across the Alameda marsh to the Oakland hills, 1899. Sailing vessels are moored on the estuary. (Courtesy of the Pat Hathaway Collection; Edgar A. Cohen photograph.)

Harbor Improvements of the U.S. Army Corps of Engineers

In its natural state, Oakland's waterfront was fringed by marsh and adjoined by tidelands which became mud flats at low tide. On the west, where the railroad maintained its port facilities, the shoreline fronted directly on the bay. To the south, a winding inlet separated the East Bay mainland from the Alameda peninsula. Originally called San Antonio Creek, this sheltered waterway is now commonly known as the estuary. A quarter-mile wide at its mouth, and some three miles in length, the estuary terminated in a broad, shallow basin. At the inlet's midpoint, an arm extended north to the base of the hills; this slough was dammed in 1869 to form Lake Merritt.

The estuary was quite shallow. Along its western reach, tidal currents carved a channel varying in depth from ten feet at low water to twenty feet at high water. A mile west of the mouth the current fanned out and deposited silts to create a bar within two feet of the surface at low tide—a navigational hazard to ferryboats and other shallow-draft vessels. In 1859, Oakland citizens raised $14,000 to dredge a makeshift channel through the bar.

For a permanent solution, the city turned to the federal government, which is authorized by the Constitution to maintain the nation's navigable waterways. Projects are undertaken at the discretion of Congress, under the direct supervision of the U.S. Army Corps of Engineers. The Corps' San Francisco District, established in 1866, originally covered the western United States and Hawaii. This vast jurisdiction was later divided into smaller districts headquartered in Portland (1871), Seattle (1896), Los Angeles (1898), Honolulu (1905), and Sacramento (1907). Today the San Francisco District takes in a strip of coastal land extending north from Big Sur to the Oregon border.

Oakland began lobbying for harbor improvements in the late 1860s, and Congress appropriated funds for a detailed study in the River and Harbor Act of 1873. Completed the following year, the engineers' report proposed a wide range of projects. Two parallel training walls, or jetties, were to be built at the mouth of the estuary, extending west through the bar into deep water. A dredged channel would run between these walls to a dredged tidal basin at the estuary's east end. Finally, a tidal canal 400 feet wide and one mile long would be cut through the neck of the Alameda peninsula, connecting the tidal basin to San Leandro Bay, where a dam with tidal gates was to be erected.

Together, these harbor improvements were intended to create a strong tidal current for scouring the channel. During high tide, water would fill San Leandro Bay and collect in the tidal basin. The dam gates at the mouth of the bay would then be closed, forcing and accelerating the ebb tide through the narrow tidal canal into the tidal basin. The combined outflow would then be funneled between the training walls, scouring the channel of silt.

It was estimated that the improvements would require thirty years and $1.8 million to complete. Despite sporadic funding from Congress and litigation with property owners, contractors completed the work on schedule, at a total cost of $2.5 million. The prime mover of the overall project, Colonel George H. Mendell, served as commanding officer of the San Francisco District of the Army Corps of Engineers, from 1871 until his retirement in 1895.

The stone training walls, erected between 1874 and 1894, extended approximately two miles into the bay. Dredging of the channels and tidal basin began in the late 1870s. By 1900, the channel had a width of 300 feet and a low-tide depth of 20 feet as far east as the Webster Street Bridge, where it divided into smaller channels. The tidal basin, within Brooklyn Basin, covered 300 acres to a depth of two feet at low water. The opening of the tidal canal in 1902 brought this first phase of harbor work to a close. Thirteen years under construction, the canal was spanned by three new bridges, at 29th Avenue–Park Street, Fruitvale Avenue, and High Street. The only component of the 1874 plan that remained unbuilt was the tidal dam, deemed unnecessary in later studies.

Excavating the tidal canal, circa 1890. Devised by the Army Corps of Engineers, this one-mile-long waterway linked the estuary to San Leandro Bay. (Courtesy of the Oakland History Room, Oakland Public Library.)

An Overview of Oakland's Waterfront and Maritime Activity

The federal harbor improvements of the late nineteenth century laid the foundation for Oakland's development as a port. Innovative hydraulic dredges removed tons of sediment from the estuary and forced the material through floating pipelines to reclaim hundreds of acres of tideland and marsh. The reconfigured shoreline, in addition to containing many new sites for development, provided the basis for legal decisions that would ultimately return the waterfront to municipal control.

Waterborne commerce along the estuary increased dramatically. Much of the activity was carried on by small sailing vessels on bay, river, and coast routes. As the shipping channel was progressively widened and deepened, oceangoing traffic through the jetties increased. Most shipping occurred west of the drawbridges at Webster and Alice Streets. These bridges were equipped with movable sections (draws) to allow vessels to pass through, but the mechanisms were slow.

By the late 1870s, square-riggers drawing seventeen feet of water were calling at wharves along the Oakland waterfront. In the 1880s, when California was the center of the American whaling industry, fleets of whaling barks began to be laid up for the winter in the estuary's protected waters. Over the years, the harbor became famous as a moorage for wooden sailing ships and, finally, as a graveyard for the decaying hulks of square-riggers.

The most celebrated of the commercial sailing fleets belonged to the Alaska Packers Association, the world's largest salmon-packing concern, whose vessels were berthed in the estuary beginning in the 1890s. A

The Alaska Packers fleet in winter moorage, Alameda, circa 1915. Also shown are the company logo and a can label from about the same period. (Courtesy of the Oakland Museum of California.)

12

mooring and maintenance facility was built on the Alameda waterfront at the turn of the century. The company's ships marked the seasons with stately ritual, heading north in the spring and returning through the Golden Gate in late summer or early fall, laden with salmon.

Improved navigation also made the estuary attractive to shipbuilders. The East Bay's first important shipyards were established in Alameda, where vacant waterfront land was plentiful. Charles G. White and Hay & Wright both moved their operations from San Francisco to Alameda in 1890, occupying marshland sites west of the Webster Street Bridge. Through the turn of the century, these well-known shipbuilders turned out dozens of wooden vessels, from river steamers to deep-water barkentines and schooners, which were used for the lumber, sugar, coal,

The estuary shipyard of Hay & Wright was one of the busiest on the coast. In this view from 1897, workers pose with the keel beam for the Charles Nelson, *a steam schooner that carried passengers to Alaska during the Klondike gold rush. (Courtesy of the Alameda Historical Museum.)*

and Klondike trades. Another respected shipbuilder, William A. Boole, opened Oakland's first all-purpose yard in 1900 at the foot of Adeline Street, on land acquired from the Oakland Waterfront Company.

Various other industries sprang up along Oakland's waterfront to process goods shipped in by rail and water. Industrialization in the Bay Area had intensified in the 1860s, when the Civil War cut off imports of manufactured goods from the East. During the 1870s, an expanding rail network made possible the location of factories in towns and cities other than San Francisco. In Oakland, lumber was used by carriage factories and planing mills; scrap iron, by foundries and machine shops; wheat, by flour mills; cotton, by cotton mills; fruits and vegetables, by canneries.

Lumberyards and coal bunkers proliferated along the estuary on land leased from the Oakland Waterfront Company. Equipped with wharves and connected by rail to the First Street freight tracks, these large storage facilities supplied building materials and fuel to Bay Area cities and inland communities. Planing mills associated with the lumberyards produced machine-milled woodwork which was also shipped over a wide region.

The railroad's waterfront monopoly meant that most freight continued to be funneled through the Oakland Long Wharf. Here great quantities of goods (principally wheat, lumber, coal, and iron) were transferred between rail cars and deep-water vessels, or transshipped to and from San Francisco via freight ferries. Wheat in particular became a major export after the Civil War, when the railroad opened up the Central Valley to large-scale farming. British barks dominated the trade, importing coal and scrap iron and carrying back grain.

Oakland's newfound prominence as a rail terminus should have guaranteed its prominence as a seaport. Ironically, the railroad's stranglehold on the waterfront inhibited such development, and the practice of transshipping goods across the bay assured the continued dominance of the Port of San Francisco. Because of the monopoly, public port facilities were virtually nonexistent in nineteenth-century Oakland. The first city-owned wharf was built in 1872 between Franklin and Webster Streets, on a small piece of land donated by the Oakland Waterfront Company. At the turn of the century, two small wharves and a few cargo sheds adjoining the Webster Street Bridge comprised the municipality's total port development. However, this would soon change.

This 1901 view, looking north from Alameda, takes in the Oakland waterfront west of the Webster Street Bridge. The estuary is lined with storage yards for lumber, coal, and building materials. Oakland's city-owned wharves adjoin the bridge, and on the far left a ferryboat is docked at the foot of Broadway. (Courtesy of the Oakland History Room, Oakland Public Library.)

Municipal Dock No. 1, Jefferson and Grove Streets, soon after its completion in 1915. Longshoremen stack crates in the traditional method of break-bulk cargo handling. The coal bunkers of Howard Terminal form a backdrop to a steamship docked at the quay wall, next to the transit shed. This site was later redeveloped as the Grove Street Pier.

CHAPTER TWO   BEGINNING OF A MUNICIPAL PORT

I n the early years of the new century, Oakland took its first steps toward the creation of a city-owned port, a move made possible by the return of the waterfront to municipal control. By World War I, the first generation of city-owned port facilities was in place. A number of other cities on the Pacific Coast, including San Francisco, Los Angeles, Portland, and Seattle, also undertook ambitious port projects during these years, all in anticipation of the 1914 opening of the Panama Canal.

The Expanding City

For Oakland, establishment of a municipal port was but one aspect of an era of remarkable prosperity. Between 1900 and 1910, the city's population increased from 67,000 to 150,000. Most of this growth followed the 1906 earthquake and San Francisco fire, which brought many residents and businesses across the bay. Annexations nearly tripled the city's area in 1909. By the end of World War I, Oakland had more than 200,000 residents, and the population would approach 300,000 over the following decade.

Served by two new transcontinental railroads, the waterfront flourished as a manufacturing and food-processing center. The Santa Fe, whose terminus was established at Richmond in 1900, extended its tracks to Oakland in 1904. The Western Pacific began service in 1910. The Realty Syndicate developed residential tracts in tandem with the electric streetcar system of the Key Route, whose three-mile-long ferry pier opened in 1903 on the western waterfront.

Under the progressive leadership of Frank K. Mott, Oakland's mayor from 1905 to 1915, voters approved bonds for parks, schools, and other projects designed to enhance the appearance and well-being of the city. Bonds also financed the establishment of a municipal port, as if to acknowledge that the "City Beautiful" could not exist without a sound economic base.

Downtown Oakland in 1925, looking east to Lake Merritt. City Hall (with cupola) and Lakeside Park are legacies of the Mayor Mott era.

The Shipping Boom

Oakland's growth and prosperity were reflected by the Bay Area at large. The region's population, which surpassed one million by World War I, supported a strong economy ranging from manufacturing to retailing. This burgeoning market was served by shipping companies that transported goods up and down the coast, across the Pacific, and through the Panama Canal. By the 1920s, maritime trade in the Bay Area had assumed the proportions of a boom. Tonnage handled by the Port of San Francisco doubled over the course of the decade, and piers became so congested that many laden vessels were diverted to the East Bay.

Larger and faster cargo vessels contributed to the boom. Improved oil-burning engines had ushered in the age of the steam-powered freighter; at the same time, steel replaced wood in ship construction. By 1900, 50 percent of the tonnage of ships built in American shipyards was of steel, and nearly 60 percent was propelled by steam. Steel-hulled steamships soon replaced square-riggers on most trade routes. Oakland's harbor statistics document the shift. In 1910, around 2,900 merchant vessels entered the estuary, evenly divided between sail and steam. Two years later, less than one-quarter were sail powered; by 1918, only 4 percent (157 of a total of 4,210). Sailing vessels would linger on as economical bulk carriers, but by World War I their day was clearly over.

Steamships on the Oakland waterfront, early 1920s.

Oakland Regains Its Waterfront

It was during this period of rapid growth in shipping that Oakland established a municipal port. In the five years following the 1906 earthquake, a stunning series of legal, political, and legislative actions returned the waterfront to municipal control. This shift in ownership allowed the Oakland Department of Public Works to institute a port development program. By 1925, when voters approved the establishment of the Port of Oakland, a dozen new facilities bordered the estuary and western waterfront.

The catalyst for change was the Western Pacific (WP), a transcontinental line seeking a terminus on San Francisco Bay. When the city granted the railroad a franchise in a tideland area adjoining the estuary's north training wall, the Southern Pacific sought an injunction in federal court. The court ruled in favor of the city and against the SP. The decision, rendered in 1907, upheld an earlier ruling that set the boundary of the SP's property at the low-tide line of 1852 (rather than the vague "shipping channel" stipulated in the original grant to Carpentier). Extensive dredging and filling associated with the federal harbor improvements had placed the 1852 line well inland. The courts affirmed the right of the city government to maintain docks and other facilities on lands lying outside the 1852 line.

The first Western Pacific train pulls into the new passenger station at Third and Washington Streets, August 1910. (Courtesy of the Oakland History Room, Oakland Public Library.)

To avoid countersuits and appeals, Mayor Mott negotiated a compromise with the Southern Pacific. The railroad agreed to relinquish its claim to the waterfront in return for a fifty-year franchise to continue its rail, ferry, and shipping operations. The company also agreed to dismantle the Oakland Long Wharf by 1918, thus providing clear access to the waterfront north of the SP's Oakland Mole, and to allow the extension of city streets beyond the railroad right-of-way on the western shoreline.

Drawn up in a formal memorandum, this compromise settlement was approved by Oakland voters as an amendment to the city charter in March 1909. Once surveys were completed establishing new bulkhead lines and new property boundaries along the 1852 low-tide line, the City Council formally ratified the settlement in November 1910. The Western Pacific had by then inaugurated service along Third Street to its new passenger station and ferry terminal.

The voters also approved a 1909 ballot measure authorizing the annexation of hundreds of acres of state-owned tidelands off the western shoreline. These submerged lands, which lay beyond the 1852 low-tide line, encompassed the Western Pacific Mole, the Southern Pacific Long Wharf and Mole, and the Key Route Pier. In May 1911, the State of California conveyed the property to the city of Oakland, providing the final victory in the waterfront wars.

The Livingston Street Pier in 1912, looking across Brooklyn Basin to Alameda and the Alaska Packers fleet. The view is now blocked by Coast Guard Island.

Municipal Port Construction

In November 1909, a full year before the City Council ratified the waterfront settlement, Oakland voters approved a $2.5 million bond issue for municipal port improvements. The program was placed under the direction of the Department of Public Works, and it was overseen by the Board of Public Works. In 1911, when a new city charter established a commission form of government, the board came under the purview of a commissioner of public works.

Colonel William H. Heuer, the district officer of the Army Corps of Engineers between 1901 and 1907, was retained as consulting engineer. The plans as adopted called for three separate projects: a bulkhead with wharves on the western waterfront, a quay wall and transit shed on the estuary near Broadway, and a pier on the estuary in East Oakland. Work began in 1910 under various contracts, and by 1915 the entire $2.5 million had been spent.

The Livingston Street Pier, situated at the east end of Brooklyn Basin, was the first of the city's projects to be built.

Completed in 1912, this small pier for lumber and general cargo was constructed of reinforced concrete for durability and fire resistance. It was the first pier on the Oakland waterfront built of this material. (The Bay Area's first concrete pier and transit shed had been erected several years earlier by the Port of San Francisco.)

The next project brought to completion was the quay wall, a massive bulkhead and dock extending one-third of a mile along the estuary waterfront between Myrtle and Clay Streets. The reinforced-concrete structure measured forty feet from top to bottom, tapering from a width of twenty-two feet at its base to eighteen inches at the top. Built in two phases between 1910 and 1914—the first contractor went bankrupt—the wall ended up costing the city about $1.4 million, principally for site acquisition. It was to have extended a full half-mile, from Myrtle Street to Broadway, but a property owner blocked construction east of Clay Street.

Because the quay wall was built inland from shore, tons of soil on the harbor side had to be removed. Subsequent dredging produced a berthing basin with a depth of twenty-seven feet at low tide. Between 1913 and 1915, soil and sediment were deposited behind the wall, creating a 150-foot-wide strip of compacted fill which was graded, paved, and equipped with spur tracks connecting with the Southern Pacific and Western Pacific tracks on First and Third Streets. The final component of the project, a steel-frame, corrugated-iron transit shed measuring 90 by 400 feet, was erected in 1915 on the paved area between Grove and Jefferson Streets. Collectively, the quay wall, pavement, shed, and basin were known as Municipal Dock No. 1, or the Jefferson Street Dock.

The quay wall under consruction, looking east from the vicinity of Market Street, circa 1913. Wood piles were bolted to the wall's harbor face to cushion docking vessels.

Interior of the quay-wall transit shed, soon after its completion in 1915.

Aerial view of the Key Route Basin on the western waterfront, circa 1920. Filling operations are underway behind the city bulkhead. The Southern Pacific Mole (left) has been shorn of the Long Wharf; the Key Route Pier (right) extends nearly to Yerba Buena Island. The Fourteenth Street trestle (center) crosses the tidelands to the Union Construction Company shipyard.

The largest and costliest of the projects called for the creation of an entirely new waterfront off Oakland's western shore, in a tideland area known as the Key Route Basin (bordered by the Southern Pacific's Long Wharf and Mole on the south and the Key Route Pier on the north). In 1911, following the city's annexation of the tidelands, work began on a rock-fill bulkhead, extending from the mole to the vicinity of the pier. Situated three-quarters of a mile offshore, this milelong rubble seawall followed the new bulkhead line and enclosed roughly 400 acres of city-owned tidelands.

Three wooden quay wharves, comprising 2,150 feet of berthing space, were built along the finished bulkhead in 1912. Wharves No. 1 and No. 2 adjoined the Long Wharf at Seventh Street. To provide access to City Wharf No. 3, at the north end of the bulkhead, Fourteenth Street was extended by trestle across the tidelands. Extensive dredging was required to create approaches for deep-water vessels, and the dredged materials (and garbage fill) were used to begin the process of reclaiming the tidelands. By 1915, the city had spent in excess of $700,000 on the western waterfront, with reclamation barely begun.

Over the following decade, the Department of Public Works undertook several other projects. Financed by the city's general fund, these later projects all utilized wood construction to reduce costs. The first to be completed, in 1916, was the reconstruction of the old municipal wharf at Franklin and Webster Streets. This was followed in 1918 by a totally new wharf and transit shed at Clay Street, known as Municipal Dock

The Market Street Pier as it appeared in 1928.

No. 2, or the Clay Street Wharf. In 1923, a new wharf for lumber and general cargo went in at the foot of Dennison Street, next to the Livingston Street Pier. The Market Street Pier of 1924, erected at a cost of about $275,000, was the most ambitious of these projects. Angling out from the quay wall a distance of 570 feet, the pier supported one of the largest transit sheds on the Oakland waterfront.

The east end of the quay wall, between Grove and Clay Streets, circa 1918. Navy vessels are docked by the transit shed, and the newly opened Clay Street Wharf is partly visible to the right. Smoke spews from a PG&E power station.

Harbor Improvements

Federal harbor improvements kept pace with Oakland's port developments. In 1910, after a decade of studies, the Army Corps of Engineers adopted a new long-range plan calling for wider and deeper shipping channels. By 1920, a channel 500 feet wide and 30 feet deep at mean low tide had been dredged from deep water in San Francisco Bay to Brooklyn Basin, a distance of nearly five miles. Within the basin the channel branched into smaller channels along the Oakland and Alameda

The waterfront in 1923.

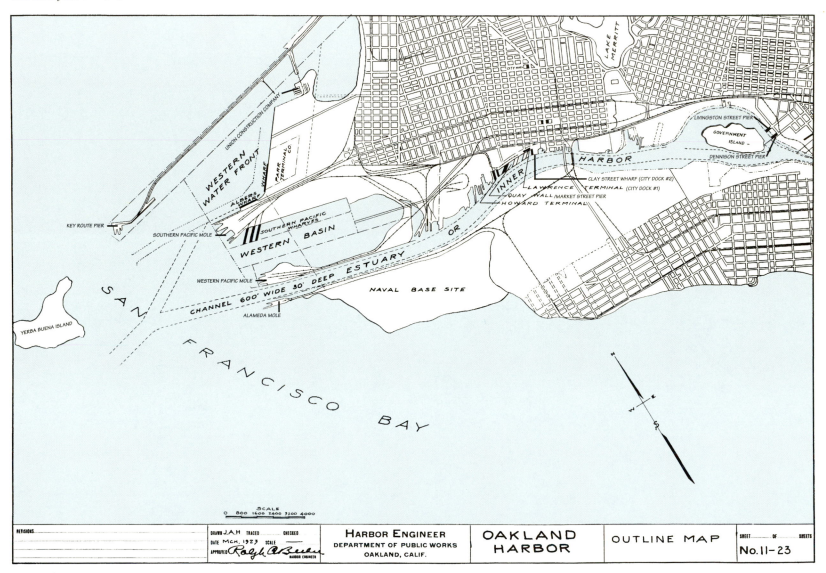

shores, each 300 feet wide and 25 feet deep, with a shallower channel continuing east through the tidal canal.

Many business leaders in the Bay Area had advocated a coordinated approach to port development as the most effective way to reap the benefits of increased shipping from the Panama Canal. In accordance with these views, Colonel Thomas H. Rees, the Army Corps district officer from 1911 to 1917, envisioned a deep-water basin extending along the East Bay waterfront from Oakland to Richmond. Although this regional scheme received strong support in Werner Hegemann's landmark 1915 study, "Report on a City Plan for the Municipalities of Oakland & Berkeley," Oakland and Richmond proceeded with separate port plans.

One by-product of the Oakland harbor work was Government Island, now known as Coast Guard Island. Created between 1915 and 1917 by depositing dredged material behind levees in Brooklyn Basin, the seventy-acre island has served successively as a shipyard, a regional center for federal agencies, and a Coast Guard base. Though it is within Alameda city limits, the island adjoins the Oakland shoreline to which it is connected by bridge.

By the 1920s, a half-century of improvements had transformed the estuary into a harbor accessible to the largest merchant vessels. The removal of the antiquated drawbridges at Webster and Harrison Streets (the latter erected in 1898 to replace the Alice Street Bridge) rid the harbor of its last major impediments to navigation. In 1923, the year the Harrison Street Bridge was dismantled, Alameda County voters approved $4.5 million in bonds for an underwater tunnel to replace the Webster Street Bridge. Opened in 1928, the Posey Tube had sufficient depth to allow thirty-five feet of clearance in the shipping channel.

1930s postcard view of the Alameda Portal of the Posey Tube.

Waterfront Developments

Oakland's improved harbor stimulated industrial growth and shipping of all sorts. Leading import items through the 1920s included lumber, building materials, iron, and oil (which replaced coal as an energy source). Grain remained an important export. Oakland also ranked as one of the state's leading exporters of canned and dried fruits. Fresh fruit was brought in by rail and truck from farm districts, processed in local canneries, and exported by rail and ship. City-owned terminals were too small to handle much of this trade, with most cargo passing through facilities owned by railroads, industries, and private operators.

The estuary's oldest privately owned cargo facility was Howard Terminal. Opened in 1900, the terminal occupied a seventeen-acre site acquired from the Oakland Waterfront Company, at the foot of Filbert Street in West Oakland. In its early years, Howard specialized in bulk commodities such as grain, lumber, and coal, and its huge coal bunkers dominated this section of the waterfront. The terminal began handling other types of cargo during World War I, and over the years its facilities grew to include transit sheds, warehouses, and a railway.

The estuary's other privately owned shipping facility was Encinal Terminals. Established in 1925 on the Alameda waterfront east of Webster Street, the complex ultimately included a large berthing basin, three transit sheds, and a railside warehouse. The terminal was developed by the California Packing Corporation (now Del Monte), on land owned by a subsidiary, the Alaska Packers

Howard Terminal, shown here in the early 1920s, provided "Service to the Seven Seas."

Association, whose maintenance yard adjoined on the east. The Alameda Belt Line, a waterfront railroad opened by Alameda's municipal government in 1918, linked Encinal Terminals to the transcontinental rail lines in Oakland.

During World War I, shipyards on both sides of the estuary enjoyed spectacular growth. The Moore Shipbuilding Company operated one of the largest plants on the coast. Originally known as Moore & Scott Iron Works, the firm moved from San Francisco to Oakland in 1909, acquiring William Boole's yard at the foot of Adeline Street. Between 1916 and 1921, Moore's 12,000 employees produced nearly sixty steel freighters and tankers, setting records for speed of construction and multiple launchings. Closely resembling Moore in size and productivity was Bethlehem's Alameda plant, one of four Bay Area shipyards owned by the steel giant. Moore (known after 1924 as Moore Dry Dock), Bethlehem, and other estuary shipyards weathered the postwar doldrums by overhauling vessels and fabricating structural steel.

Launching of the 7,100-ton turbine steamer Thordis *at Oakland's Moore shipyard, January 1917. (Courtesy of the San Francisco Maritime National Historical Park, W. A. Muhlman Collection.)*

Looking north to Oakland from Alameda, late 1920s. Brooklyn Basin and Government Island form a backdrop for Encinal Terminals and the Alaska Packers yard. (Courtesy of the Alameda Historical Museum.)

The Businesses of Oakland's Municipal Port

The city of Oakland leased its port facilities to a mix of tenants. By World War I, lessees on the western waterfront included a grain distributor, a terminal operator, and a shipbuilder. The Department of Public Works continued to manage the city's estuary facilities until about 1920, when most of these docks and sheds were also let to private firms. The Lawrence Warehouse Company carried on general-cargo operations at Municipal Docks No. 1 and No. 2 (Dock No. 1 became known as Lawrence Terminal).

Albers Milling Company, circa 1920. The high cost of contract dredging led the city to purchase its own dredge, which is shown here.

On the western waterfront, Albers Milling Company, a leading exporter and distributor of grain, feed, and flour, leased a five-acre tract adjoining the Southern Pacific Mole and City Wharf No. 1. By 1918, the site contained an eight-story mill building and warehouse. Albers later became a subsidiary of Carnation, and the mill would be enlarged and rebuilt several times.

The Union Construction Company occupied a large parcel of city-owned tideland at the end of the Fourteenth Street trestle, near City Wharf No. 3. Union's shipyard, constructed in 1918–19, went into production as the war ended. Subleased in the early 1920s to the Pacific Coast Engineering Company, the property eventually became part of the Oakland Army Base.

As the remnant of the Oakland Long Wharf was being demolished, Parr Terminal Company negotiated a lease for seventy acres of reclaimed tideland that would adjoin Seventh Street and City Wharf No. 2. Opened in the summer of 1920, Parr's new quay wharf and transit shed provided 1,500 feet of berthing space and 60,000 square feet of enclosed storage. The transit shed, measuring 120 by 500 feet, was Oakland's largest, and the first on the waterfront to be built of reinforced concrete. An array of electrical and mechanical equipment facilitated the handling of all types of packaged and bulk cargo.

Following the construction of a pier for tankers north of the quay wharf in the mid-1920s, Parr Terminal also became an important oil distribution center, with storage facilities operated by Richfield and Texaco. Parr's other industrial tenants included a steel foundry, a machine works, a vegetable-oil refinery, and sulphur and nitrate companies.

In 1925, Parr was the most up-to-date cargo facility on the waterfront—a model for the Port of Oakland as it began the task of building a new generation of marine terminals to meet the needs of modern shipping.

Parr Terminal in the early 1920s. Tugboats escort a square-rigger past steamships docked at the transit shed.

Union Construction Company shipyard, Armistice Day, 1918. The Fourteenth Street trestle is partially visible on the right.

UNION CONSTRUCTION COMPANY

ENGINEERS AND SHIPBUILDERS

MAIN OFFICE AND WORKS
KEY ROUTE BASIN FOOT OF 14TH STREET
OAKLAND, CALIFORNIA

PO N⁰ 102
5 23 28

The Port of Oakland's Grove Street Pier opened in 1928 between Grove and Jefferson Streets, on the site of Municipal Dock No. 1. In this view, a steamship from the Luckenbach Line is docked alongside the east section of the pier's double transit shed. The site now forms part of the Charles P. Howard Container Terminal.

CHAPTER THREE   THE PORT OF OAKLAND

O akland and other West Coast ports felt the full effect of the Panama Canal in the 1920s, a decade of prosperity following world war and recession. The canal opened up new trade routes to the Gulf of Mexico, the East Coast of the United States, South America, and Europe. Coastwise trade and Pacific trade flourished as well. This rising tide of cargo, much of it carried by modern steamships requiring larger berths and more time for loading and discharging, threatened to overwhelm the capacity of the Bay Area's ports.

In 1925, at the height of the shipping boom, Oakland voters approved bonds for an expanded municipal port overseen by an autonomous Board of Port Commissioners. Officially established in 1927, the Port of Oakland rapidly developed new terminals to accommodate larger cargo vessels. With relatively few changes, these facilities would serve the Port over the next four decades, until the advent of containerized shipping.

Establishing the Port of Oakland

Late in 1924, the Oakland City Council appointed a board of three consulting engineers to formulate the city's first long-range plan for port development. The board consisted of Gustave B. Hegardt, manager of the Commission of Public Docks in Portland, Oregon; Charles T. Leeds, consulting engineer to the Port of Los Angeles; and Charles D. Marx, a professor of engineering at Stanford University.

In their "Report on Port of Oakland," completed in September 1925, the engineers provided an overview of existing facilities, analyzed current problems, and made recommendations for future development. Priority was given to four new projects: a wharf and transit shed on the western waterfront at the end of Fourteenth Street; a pier with double transit shed on the estuary between Grove and Jefferson Streets; an identical pier and shed nearby, between Clay and Washington Streets; and a similar but larger facility on Brooklyn Basin between Thirteenth and Fourteenth Avenues. Total cost of construction for these projects, including dredging and contingencies, was estimated at $9,960,000.

The engineers also recommended that port administration be "vested in a board or commission of competent, responsible men, serving without compensation and free from political interference"—a veiled reference to the political controversy surrounding the report. Mayor John L. Davie and his allies opposed expansion of the municipal port, believing that Oakland could not compete with San Francisco; instead, the waterfront should be given over to private industry. The supporters of expansion were led by Leroy R. Goodrich, Oakland's commissioner of public works and the city's principal advocate of port development and port autonomy.

On November 10, 1925, Oakland voters overwhelmingly approved the issuance of $9,960,000 in bonds for the specified improvements. The terms of the bond issue required the creation of a Board of Port Commissioners, made up of "five representative businessmen of the city," who were to be appointed by the mayor and ratified by the City Council. A temporary board took office in December 1925, becoming permanent under a charter amendment passed in December 1926. Five men were then appointed to staggered six-year terms. Attorney Roscoe D. Jones, pharmacist Robert A. Leet, department store owner H. C. Capwell, and tobacconist Ben F. Pendleton were holdovers from the temporary board. The new member was George C. Pardee, a former mayor and state governor. The permanent board was officially sworn in on February 12, 1927, with Jones serving as its first president.

The Board of Port Commissioners oversaw a new and independent arm of city government known as the Port of Oakland. The commissoners were given plenary power to build, equip, and maintain facilities, and to control revenues generated by their operation. All city-owned shoreline properties, including marine terminals formerly managed by the Department of Public Works, now formed part of an official Port Area under the jurisdiction of the Port of Oakland.

Gustave B. Hegardt

Administration and Management

Following its permanent appointment, the Board of Port Commissioners rented office space in the Oakland Bank Building, at Twelfth Street and Broadway. This downtown location served the Port during the early phase of construction. In 1931, the offices were moved to the Grove Street Pier, the largest of the new transit sheds and the one closest to the central business district. Overlooking the waterfront from the shed's mezzanine floors were the commissioners' board room, the offices of the port manager and his assistant, and the engineering, traffic, purchasing, accounting, and legal departments. The Port's headquarters would remain here until 1961, when they were moved several blocks east to Jack London Square.

Gustave B. Hegardt served as the Port of Oakland's first manager and chief engineer. A coauthor of the "Report on Port of Oakland," he had been appointed to the position in March 1926 by the interim Board of Port Commissioners. At the same time, Arthur H. Abel was hired as his assistant. Following Hegardt's retirement in 1932, Abel took over the position, which he held until his own retirement in 1952. These two men were chiefly responsible for the development of the Port of Oakland during its first twenty-five years.

Born in Sweden in 1859, Gustave Hegardt came to the United States as a boy. A graduate of several technical schools, he began his career in Illinois with the Army Corps of Engineers, joining the Corps' Portland District in 1888 to supervise construction of locks, jetties, and fortifications on the Columbia River. Hegardt left the Corps around 1905 to start a consulting firm in Portland, specializing in land surveys, irrigation systems, and reclamation projects. In 1911, he was appointed chief engineer and manager of the newly established Portland Commission of Public Docks—later to merge with the Port of Portland—where he would remain fifteen years, overseeing a $10.5 million construction program.

Arthur Abel was born in 1882 in Walla Walla, Washington, and received a degree in civil engineering from Washington State College. After working briefly as a railroad surveyor, he became a draftsman at Hegardt's Portland firm. Abel followed Hegardt to the Portland Commission of Public Docks, where he served as his assistant, and in the spring of 1926 accompanied him south from Oregon to California.

Board of Port Commissioners, 1937. Seated, left to right: Eugene W. Roland, Ralph T. Fisher, President James J. McElroy, George C. Pardee, and Frank Colbourn. Standing behind McElroy are Port Manager Arthur H. Abel and Port Attorney Merkell C. Baer.

Construction Program and Harbor Improvements

In Oakland, Hegardt and Abel quickly assembled a staff to begin the design process. The first construction contract was awarded in the summer of 1926, and by 1931 most of the improvements outlined in the "Report on Port of Oakland" were completed. New facilities consisted of two quay wharves and two piers with a total berthing space of 5,750 feet; six transit sheds enclosing over 500,000 square feet; and four warehouses comprising nearly 650,000 square feet.

For planning purposes, the waterfront was divided into districts. The estuary became the Inner Harbor. The western waterfront was partitioned into three areas, known as the Outer Harbor, Middle Harbor, and North Harbor. The Outer Harbor consisted of the old Key Route Basin, stretching from the Southern Pacific Mole to the Key Route Pier. To the south, between the Southern Pacific and Western Pacific Moles, lay the Middle Harbor. Extending north from the Key Route Pier to the Emeryville city limit was the North Harbor. The Port limited new construction to the Inner and Outer Harbors, holding the Middle and North Harbors in reserve for future development.

The Port of Oakland built relatively few waterfront facilities after 1931. New construction through World War II included two transit-shed additions, three warehouses, and about 2,000 feet of berthing space. The original $9.96 million in bond monies was depleted by 1938. Between 1934 and 1940, the Public Works Administration, the Works Progress Administration, and other federal agencies provided a total of $2.35 million for various Port projects. After World War II, construction was financed by Port revenues and bonds.

Throughout this period, the Army Corps of Engineers continued to oversee channel dredging to accommodate large merchant vessels (few of which exceeded 30 feet in draft). By 1930, both the Inner and Outer Harbors had 30-foot channels varying in width from 400 to 600 feet. During World War II, the military deepened the Outer Harbor channel to 35 feet. These channel depths would be

Transit shed interior, Grove Street Pier, 1930s.

34

maintained until the 1970s. Other harbor improvements from this period included the replacement of two obsolete drawbridges on the tidal canal as well as the removal of abandoned sailing vessels from the estuary. Beginning in 1934, the Port surveyed the harbor for hulks and instituted abatement proceedings; by World War II, the square-riggers were gone.

New Types of Facilities

Maritime facilities erected by the Port of Oakland shared common features of design and construction. Durability and fire resistance were paramount concerns. Piers and wharves had reinforced-concrete decks. Steel-framed and reinforced-concrete transit sheds were equipped with firewalls, rolling steel doors, and automatic sprinklers. Due to this type of construction and level of protection, the Port of Oakland was able to secure fire insurance rates which were among the lowest for the nation's ports.

Functionally, the terminals were designed to expedite the movement of cargo and to avoid congestion in the harbor. When the site was of sufficient size, quay wharves running parallel to shore were utilized to permit easy docking and departure. Berths accommodated vessels up to 500 feet in length, with wide aprons for shipside trackage, trucks, and other vehicles. Rail spurs and paved roads linked the terminals to main lines and highways. Large transit sheds enabled goods to be stored with little or no stacking, and to be moved quickly between ship and rail car via doorways on the dock and land sides. The sheds were designed expressly for the circulation of trucks, which could enter at one end and exit at the other, without having to turn around.

To these practical considerations was added a concern for architectural beauty. The "Report on Port of Oakland" recommended that "for aesthetic and advertising value, the shore and pierhead ends of sheds should be finished with some regard for architecture." This was already a common practice at the Port of San Francisco. As built, Oakland's new transit sheds had similar fronts that conveyed a neoclassical

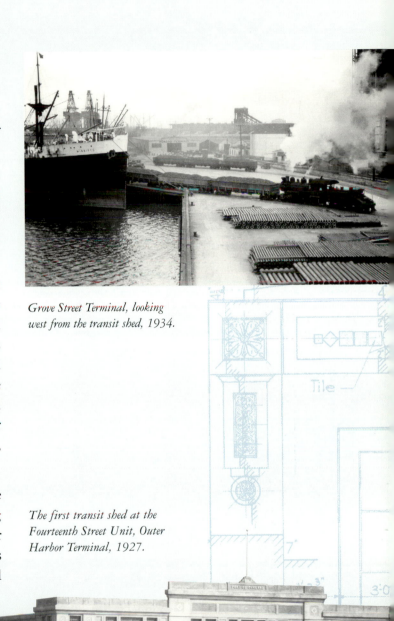

Grove Street Terminal, looking west from the transit shed, 1934.

The first transit shed at the Fourteenth Street Unit, Outer Harbor Terminal, 1927.

Map of the Outer Harbor, 1945. Numbered facilities include the Fourteenth Street Unit (2); Oil Pier (3); Seventh Street Unit (4); Albers Milling Company (5); and Southern Pacific Mole (6).

feeling through their symmetrical arrangement of piers, cornices, ornamental panels, and openings. This aesthetic approach to utilitarian structures was one facet of the City Beautiful Movement, which promoted civic order through the careful design and siting of buildings and other urban features. Oakland participated in this national movement in various ways, as exemplified by its City Hall, schools, parks, and municipal port buildings.

Outer Harbor Terminal

The Port of Oakland's largest maritime facility prior to containerization was the Outer Harbor Terminal—the city's shipping center for outbound general cargo, inbound petroleum products, and various other bulk commodities. This complex of three adjoining terminals (Fourteenth Street to the north, Seventh Street on the south, and the Oil Pier between) contained more than a mile of berthing space, and was capable of handling ten or more oceangoing vessels at a time. Dozens of steamship lines called there regularly.

As noted in the previous chapter, the city began developing this section of the waterfront in the 1910s by constructing a bulkhead, filling in tidelands, and leasing tracts to various tenants. Prior to 1927, when the Port opened its first terminal in the Outer Harbor, shipping and industrial activity on the western waterfront were limited to private enterprise. The two largest leaseholds, Parr Terminal and Union Construction, reverted to Port ownership in 1933.

The Port of Oakland acquired Parr Terminal after Parr gave up its lease and relocated to the Port of Richmond, where it had been developing new terminals since the mid-1920s. Under Port ownership, Parr's Outer Harbor facilities became known as the Seventh Street Unit and the Oil Pier. The Seventh Street Unit, with its three-berth quay wharf and transit shed, handled bulk items like scrap metal, mineral ores, and fertilizers. The Oil Pier, linked by pipeline to onshore tanks,

The Fourteenth Street Unit as it appeared in the mid-1930s, looking north to the old Union Construction shipyard basin. The terminal's two transit sheds are adjoined by five warehouses.

could berth two tankers at a time. The Port periodically enlarged both facilities, which were adjoined by industrial tenants dealing in metals, chemicals, petroleum products, and vegetable oils.

The Fourteenth Street Unit, the Port's principal terminal for outbound general cargo, was a totally new facility, built in phases between 1926 and 1936. In completed form, it included a six-berth quay wharf, two transit sheds, and five warehouses. The opening of the wharf and transit shed, in November 1927, was the occasion for a special dockside ceremony, since these were the first maritime facilities completed by the Port of Oakland. A wharf extension and a second shed were placed in operation in 1930, and the terminal was extended to the north several times through 1936. The old Union Construction shipyard basin provided ample shoreline acreage for expansion.

The five warehouses at the Fourteenth Street Unit were constructed between 1929 and 1934. Four of these buildings were operated under lease by two private firms: Rosenberg Bros. & Company, and Libby, McNeill & Libby—the world's largest shippers, respectively, of dried fruits and canned foods. Rosenberg leased the row of three warehouses behind Transit Shed No. 1; Libby occupied a single warehouse adjoining Transit Shed No. 2. The fifth warehouse (to the north) was operated by the Port as a storage facility for agricultural products awaiting shipment. Rosenburg and Libby provided most of the outbound cargo at the Outer Harbor. This export trade attracted numerous steamship lines, generating revenues for the terminal's continual expansion.

Oakland's Outer Harbor, 1939. The Fourteenth Street Unit, Oil Pier, and Seventh Street Unit are adjoined by the Albers Milling Company and Southern Pacific Mole (right).

The Inner Harbor

The Port's three new facilities on the estuary—the Grove Street Terminal, the Ninth Avenue Terminal, and the Inland Waterways Terminal—were opened between 1928 and 1931. They were operated in conjunction with the existing piers and sheds at Market, Clay, Livingston, and Dennison Streets. Two of the Inner Harbor facilities recommended in the "Report on Port of Oakland" (at Clay and Washington Streets, and at Thirteenth and Fourteenth Avenues) were never built due to property disputes.

The Grove Street Pier projected from the quay wall between Jefferson Street and Grove Street (now Martin Luther King, Jr., Way). Built between 1926 and 1928, the three-berth pier and U-shaped transit shed occupied the site of Municipal Dock No. 1, necessitating the removal of the old transit shed from the quay wall. The Grove Street Pier, Market Street Pier, Clay Street Wharf, and quay-wall dock were operated as a single unit called the Grove Street Terminal. This facility could

In this aerial view from about 1930, downtown Oakland and the hills form a backdrop for the Grove Street Terminal. Projecting from the quay wall are the Market Street Pier and the Grove Street Pier with its double transit shed.

accommodate seven oceangoing vessels at a time and was regularly used by ten or more steamship lines. Its central location adjacent to Oakland's wholesaling and warehousing district made it a convenient shipping point for a wide variety of inbound and outbound commodities.

The Ninth Avenue Terminal, which opened in 1930 at the west end of Brooklyn Basin, took the place of the planned but unbuilt pier at Thirteenth and Fourteenth Avenues. Developed in stages between 1929 and 1938, Ninth Avenue ultimately included a five-berth quay wharf, transit shed, paved storage yards, and land for industrial tenants. Acreage acquired in 1936 allowed the Port to extend the facility westward and provide land for lease. The terminal served several intercoastal and coastwise lines. Its paved yards were suitable for handling lumber and other bulk commodities, and the principal tenants through the 1950s were lumber companies.

The Inland Waterways Terminal jutted into the estuary at the end of Webster Street, on the site of Oakland's first municipal wharf. Erected by the Port in 1931, this pier and transit shed were operated under lease by the Bay Cities Transportation Company. The terminal received produce and other commodities brought in by river barge and steamer from the interior valleys, and it also funneled goods back to the state's interior. Inbound produce was distributed to the nearby warehouses and wholesale vendors of the Oakland Produce Market, transferred to the adjacent Haslett cold-storage warehouse, or transshipped to other terminals.

Ninth Avenue Terminal in the late 1930s, during expansion of the quay wharf.

The Inland Waterways Terminal in the 1950s. (Courtesy of the Oakland History Room, Oakland Public Library.)

Trade

The Port of Oakland enjoyed a rapidly expanding volume of business in its early years. In 1929, the U.S. Treasury Department designated Oakland a full port of entry and established local customs service. Through legal action and appeal to federal authorities, the Port gradually overturned discriminatory shipping practices promulgated by the Port of San Francisco and certain steamship lines. In 1932, the double fee that had long been charged by harbor pilots bringing vessels to Oakland was eliminated. Two years later, Oakland was opened to selected ships traveling to and from the Far East.

By the mid-1930s, the Port of Oakland was a regular port of call for more than forty steamship lines. Trade routes extended up and down the coast, across the Pacific, and through the Panama Canal to the Gulf of Mexico, the Caribbean, South America, the Atlantic seaboard, and Europe. Virtually all of this shipping was cargo related, with limited passenger service on some lines.

Steamships docked at the Outer Harbor's Fourteenth Street Unit, 1930s.

A Japanese freighter takes on scrap iron at the Seventh Street Unit, Outer Harbor Terminal, circa 1935.

Longshoremen discharging nuts imported from Brazil, Outer Harbor, 1930s.

The Port's tributary territory took in Northern California and portions of Nevada and Utah. Railroads, highways, and rivers linked Oakland to these markets. The hinterland imported wholesale and retail goods and exported agricultural and mineral products. The urban East Bay was also a major source of trade. In addition to various wholesalers and retailers, there were hundreds of industrial plants which depended on imported materials in order to process and manufacture goods for export.

Dried and canned fruits and canned vegetables, destined primarily for Europe, were Oakland's principal export items. Mineral ores, scrap iron, fabricated steel, glass products, chemicals, raw cotton, cotton fabrics, salt, refined sugar, rice, walnuts, almonds, and other food products were also exported in large quantities. The East Bay assembly plants of Chevrolet, Durant, Willys, Fageol, and Caterpillar shipped out automobiles, buses, trucks, and tractors; other companies produced automotive products such as engines, valves, batteries, tires, and springs. Clorox bleach, Calo dog food, and Golden Glow beer were all made in Oakland and sold nationally.

Commodities imported in bulk included gasoline, fuel oil, lumber, sand, cement, sulphur, fertilizer, and copra (dried coconut meat from which coconut oil is made).

San Joaquin Valley cotton in Warehouse C, pending shipment from the Fourteenth Street Unit, 1931.

Loading an Oakland-made Chevrolet at the Grove Street Pier, 1934.

41

Paper, iron, and steel were also major import items. Hundreds of tons of newsprint paper from the Pacific Northwest were consumed weekly by East Bay newspapers. Retailers, including giants like Montgomery Ward and Safeway, imported a myriad of items on a regular basis.

Each cargo had different requirements for handling. Bulk copra, for example, was unloaded from holds with suction hoses and deposited in dockside hoppers for transfer to rail cars and trucks. The stowage, discharge, and storage of break-bulk cargo (cargo broken down into small units, such as cases of canned fruit or rolls of newsprint) utilized a variety of mechanical aids to expedite the process, including shipboard derricks and land-based tractors and trailers. Forklifts and standardized pallets became widespread after World War II. Yet break-bulk cargo handling remained a slow and laborious process, and gangs of skilled stevedores might take as long as three weeks to discharge and load a freighter.

Discharging copra at Seventh Street, Outer Harbor, 1938.

Longshoremen handling rolls of newsprint, 1946.

Break-bulk operations in the 1950s.

42

For many years all cargo passing through Port of Oakland terminals was handled by Port employees (the sole exception was the Inland Waterways Terminal). In the 1930s, the Port's work force of longshoremen averaged about 175 unionized men. Occasionally there were walkouts. The waterfront strike of 1934, which shut down shipping on the West Coast for about two months, prompted officials to station armed police and soldiers at Port of Oakland facilities.

Teamsters occupied an increasingly important place in the labor force as highway and bridge construction enhanced the role of trucks in regional freight hauling. Particularly important in this regard was the San Francisco–Oakland Bay Bridge, opened in 1936 along the Bay Area's most heavily traveled corridor. This bridge, which led to the demise of the transbay ferry system, brought about a sharp increase in trucking at the Port of Oakland. The bridge's approach and east span paralleled the Key Route Pier at the north edge of the Outer Harbor Terminal, and an overpass provided a direct link between bridge and terminal. The overpass was officially opened in 1938 by a motorcade escorting President Roosevelt from Treasure Island to a Navy cruiser berthed at the Outer Harbor.

Soldiers keep watch at the Outer Harbor Terminal during the 1934 waterfront strike.

Despite a depressed world economy, the Port of Oakland enjoyed steady growth during the 1930s. In 1928, the Port handled 316,377 tons of cargo; by 1941, the figure approached 1.2 million tons. The Port's share of cargo passing through Oakland's harbor grew from less than 15 percent to nearly 60 percent during this same period. Competition came from various sources. In addition to Howard Terminal and Encinal Terminals, as well as a number of industrial plants equipped with wharves, the railroads continued to ferry large quantities of freight across the bay. Oakland remained the Bay Area's second busiest general-cargo port after San Francisco, followed by the newly developed Port of Richmond. The site of a huge Standard Oil refinery, Richmond ranked as the region's leading port for petroleum products.

This view from the early 1930s shows one of the towers of the Bay Bridge under construction, with the piers and sheds of the Port of San Francisco in the background.

The Oakland Naval Supply Depot as it appeared shortly after World War II. The Southern Pacific Mole and Albers Milling Company are in the foreground.

World War II

The bombing of Pearl Harbor late in 1941 thrust the United States into global war. Mobilization galvanized the Bay Area. The infusion of federal dollars created jobs for hundreds of thousands of new residents in the region's factories, shipyards, and military bases.

The war transformed Oakland into one of the nation's busiest military ports. Two bases on the western waterfront, covering hundreds of acres of former tidelands, were commissioned within days of Pearl Harbor. The Oakland Naval Supply Depot (later known as the Naval Supply Center and finally as the Fleet & Industrial Supply Center, Oakland) spread over the Port's Middle Harbor area. The Oakland Army Base wrapped around the Outer Harbor Terminal. Extensively developed with berths, rail spurs, transit sheds, and warehouses, both bases played major roles as staging points and supply depots for American forces in the Pacific.

During the war, the military also occupied most of the Port of Oakland's maritime facilities. Beginning in 1941, the Outer Harbor Terminal functioned as part of the Oakland Army Base, and in 1943 the Ninth Avenue Terminal was taken over by the Pacific Naval Air Bases Command. Only the Grove Street Terminal remained under Port control.

Wartime industry assumed dramatic form in the shipyards. Lining the estuary waterfronts of Oakland and Alameda were a dozen new or reactivated yards, including Moore, Bethlehem, General Engineering & Drydock, Pacific Coast Engineering, United Engineering, Pacific Bridge, and Stone. These plants employed tens of thousands of workers in the production of hundreds of new vessels, ranging from cargo ships and troop transports to minesweepers, submarine chasers, and oceangoing tugs. Thousands of battle-scarred ships were repaired here as well. Moore employed nearly 40,000 workers in an expanded plant covering 128 acres. Most of the East Bay shipyards closed soon after the war ended in 1945.

A train carrying tanks past the Grove Street Pier, 1943.

Servicemen at the Southern Pacific Mole, 1943.

Postwar Continuity

The Port of Oakland resumed control of its marine terminals within a year or two of the war's end (though military land on the western waterfront would not begin to revert to Port ownership until the 1990s). Despite ambitious plans, maritime operations underwent relatively few changes through the early 1960s. New facilities included additions at Ninth Avenue and an expanded chemical terminal in the Outer Harbor. Most of the Port's energies during this period were applied to airport growth, industrial park development, and waterfront tourism.

During the war, Port Manager Abel and his staff had begun work on a new long-range development plan. Maritime goals included a major expansion of the Outer Harbor Terminal, large-scale development of the North Harbor area, various new piers and sheds along the Inner Harbor, and a mammoth terminal complex on San Leandro Bay. While these projects represented official Port policy into the 1960s, they remained unbuilt due to their high development costs and their rapid obsolescence as the Port began restructuring its facilities to handle containers.

The postwar conservatism in maritime practices was also due to a change in leadership. Following Abel's retirement in 1952, Dudley W. Frost became the first non-engineer to head the Port of Oakland (his title—"executive director"—reflected the change). A parking consultant with close ties to Oakland's business community, Frost had served on the Board of Port Commissioners since 1946, most recently as its president. In his ten years as executive director, he placed a priority on real estate and aviation projects.

One lasting change in maritime operations from this period occurred in 1956, when the Port instituted its current practice of leasing all terminals to outside operators (as the Department of Public Works had done in the 1920s). Howard Terminal initially took over operations at the Grove Street Terminal; the Outer Harbor and Ninth Avenue Terminals were first leased to Encinal Terminals. By the early 1960s, the Port was handling 2.5 million tons of cargo annually.

During its first several decades, the Port of Oakland resembled many other mid-sized ports of the era. Its facilities, which comprised about two miles of berthing space and about twenty acres of covered storage, represented only a fraction of the capacity of the Port of San Francisco. Within a few years, a bold experiment would catapult Oakland into the front ranks of world ports.

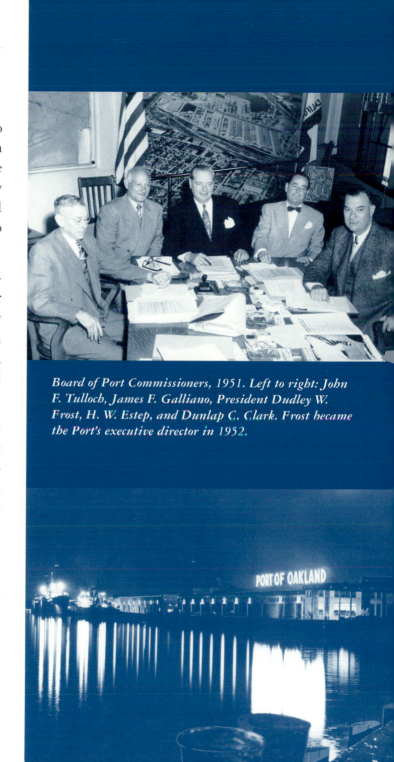

Board of Port Commissioners, 1951. Left to right: John F. Tulloch, James F. Galliano, President Dudley W. Frost, H. W. Estep, and Dunlap C. Clark. Frost became the Port's executive director in 1952.

Container cranes at the Port of Oakland's Charles P. Howard Terminal tower over a loaded ship from the Korean-flag Cho Yang Line. Opened in 1982 and enlarged in 1995, this two-berth, four-crane facility occupies the sites of the Port's Grove Street Terminal and the privately owned Howard Terminal.

CHAPTER FOUR   THE INTERMODAL ERA

Containerized shipping is the most far-reaching change in cargo handling in modern times. Developed in the United States in the 1950s, the new technology transformed shipping worldwide through the use of standardized steel containers which are carried by ship, truck, and train. Cranes and other dockside equipment move the containers between ocean and land carriers. The overall process is known as "intermodalism" because it links various modes of transport in one integrated system.

Under Executive Director Ben E. Nutter, the Port of Oakland became one of the pioneers of large-scale containerization in the 1960s. As a world leader in intermodalism, Oakland quickly overtook San Francisco as the region's leading port. By the 1980s, with most available sites along the waterfront developed for container operations, Oakland began to lose trade to other West Coast ports. Current plans call for deeper channels, expanded terminals on newly acquired military property, and improved rail and highway connections to keep the Port of Oakland competitive in a global market.

The Intermodal Revolution

Containers brought mechanized speed to cargo handling. Earlier mechanical devices such as conveyor belts and forklifts had facilitated cargo movement, but longshoremen still spent as much as three weeks discharging and loading a vessel. With the advent of high-speed container cranes, a ship's turnaround time was reduced to as little as sixteen hours. This breakthrough led to the rapid development of intermodal shipping among the world's major trading nations.

Two American steamship lines, Sea-Land and Matson, pioneered the intermodal concept. Each developed a system tailored to its needs. In 1956, Sea-Land Services, of New Jersey, began stowing cargo in steel boxes ("sea chests") which could be detached from a truck chassis and carried aboard ship. Because it served many ports, Sea-Land used shipboard cranes to move its containers. Matson, which introduced containerization to the Pacific Coast in 1958, utilized more expensive land-based cranes because it called at only a few ports.

Unable to secure a site at its home port in San Francisco, Matson based its container operations at Encinal Terminals in Alameda. There, on January 7, 1959, the world's first high-speed dockside container crane was placed in operation. Based on

Shipboard cranes on the Elizabethport, *Sea-Land Terminal, Oakland, early 1960s.*

Matson's specifications, the crane was designed and built by the Pacific Coast Engineering Company (Paceco), an East Bay firm that had moved from Oakland's Outer Harbor to Alameda during World War II. Dockside cranes proved more cost-effective than shipboard cranes, and quickly became the industry standard.

Widespread containerization on the Pacific Coast was made possible by the Mechanization and Modernization Agreement, enacted in 1961 by the International Longshoremen's & Warehousemen's Union (ILWU) and the Pacific Maritime Association. In exchange for a variety of workers' benefits, the agreement allowed steamship companies and stevedoring (cargo-handling) contractors to introduce containerized cargo and other labor-saving procedures.

Container Operations

Container terminals and traditional break-bulk terminals have quite different functional requirements. Break-bulk facilities require dockside transit sheds to store cargo awaiting shipment. Container terminals utilize dockside cranes and expanses of pavement for vehicle circulation and the storage of containers, which do not need protection from the weather. Freight stations receive goods for loading into containers; interchange areas transfer containers to and from trucks or trains. A site previously developed for break-bulk cargo is incompatible with a fully containerized terminal (though some terminals may combine both types of cargo handling). When a complete conversion occurs, transit sheds are removed and wharves and storage areas are rebuilt to withstand increased loads from cranes and stacked containers.

The world's first high-speed dockside container crane, Encinal Terminals, Alameda, 1959.

Steel containers ("boxes") come in various types and sizes. In addition to the general-purpose dry box, there are refrigerated, ventilated, bulk-liquid, and other specialized types.

Post-Panamax cranes at Yusen Terminal.

48

Though sizes vary, most containers are twenty feet or forty feet long. The standard measure of capacity is the Twenty-foot Equivalent Unit (TEU). A forty-foot container, for example, is equal to two TEUs.

Early containerships were converted break-bulk vessels with a 500–1,000 TEU capacity. By the 1970s, containerships employed "cellular" construction, i.e., they were designed from the keel up to carry stacks of containers below deck and on deck. These second-generation vessels were typically 700 feet in length, and carried 1,500 to 2,500 TEUs. The 1980s Panamax Class (of maximum size to use the Panama Canal) stretches 860 feet, with a 2,500–3,000 TEU capacity. The fourth generation, introduced in 1988, is termed Post-Panamax because it is too large for the Panama Canal. These vessels, which are 900 to 1,000 feet in length and 130 feet or more abeam, can haul 3,500 to 5,000 TEUs.

Rows of immense gantry cranes are the signposts of a major container port like Oakland. Usually rail-mounted to allow movement along the dock, the cranes load and unload boxes at great speed, using cables attached to a long horizontal boom. As container vessels have grown larger, and the on-deck stacking of containers higher, dockside cranes have become more massive. Post-Panamax cranes (capable of serving Post-Panamax vessels) are taller than a ten-story building, with an outreach over the water of 150 feet or more and a lifting capacity in excess of fifty tons. Other types of specialized equipment, including straddle carriers, front-end and top-pick loaders, and rail-mounted stacking cranes, allow containers to be moved and stored within the yard.

Front-end picker.

Crane operations.

Board of Port Commissioners, 1971. Standing, left to right: H. Boyd Gainor, Robert E. Mortensen, Executive Director Ben E. Nutter, Ted Connolly, and Thomas L. Berkley. Seated, left to right: Peter M. Tripp, William Walters, and President Y. Charles Soda.

Ben E. Nutter

Shoichi Kuwata

Containerization in Oakland

Beginning in 1962 with Sea-Land, the Port of Oakland introduced large-scale container operations to the Pacific Basin. By the end of the decade, Oakland handled the second largest volume of containers among world ports after New York. By the early 1980s, most of the Port's older maritime facilities had been replaced by a complex of container terminals operated under lease by various stevedoring companies and steamship lines.

Oakland's annual cargo volume grew from 2.5 million tons in 1962 to nearly 4 million tons in 1968, some 40 percent of it containerized. The Port reached 6.5 million tons in 1972, exceeding 12 million tons by the 1980s. For much of the decade, Oakland remained the largest container port on the Pacific Coast, second largest in the nation, and sixth in world importance in terms of container cargo. Operating revenues increased tenfold, to nearly $50 million.

The person most responsible for this dramatic growth was Ben E. Nutter, the Port of Oakland's executive director from 1962 to 1977. A natural leader, he orchestrated the shift to containers with considerable skill. Born in Kansas in 1911, Nutter grew up in Los Angeles and earned a degree in civil engineering from Oregon State College. He resided in Hawaii from 1941 to 1957, serving with the Army Corps of Engineers prior to his appointment as superintendent of public works for the islands. Nutter came to the Port of Oakland in 1957 as chief engineer, rising to the position of assistant executive director in 1959. He succeeded Dudley Frost on July 1, 1962; several months later, Sea-Land inaugurated containership service.

Nutter brought containerization to Oakland through persistent negotiation, careful planning, and a grasp of political and financial realities. He worked closely with the Board of Port Commissioners, including them in numerous trade missions and negotiations in the United States, Europe, and Asia. In 1963, he made the first of many visits to Japan, which was then preparing to make a major investment in containerization. Soon maritime officials from that country began visiting Oakland. In 1965, Nutter recruited Shoichi Kuwata, a retired Japanese shipping executive, to serve as the Port's first Far East representative. In 1968, following two years of intensive negotiations in competition with the Port of San Francisco,

Nutter and Kuwata persuaded six Japanese steamship companies to base their U.S. container operations at the Port of Oakland.

Nutter relied on revenue bonds as an effective means of financing projects. Unlike general-obligation bonds, which are retired by an increase in the tax rate, revenue bonds are paid back with revenues generated by the funded project. Their sale does not require voter approval. Authorized by a 1953 amendment to the city charter, revenue bonds were first issued by the Port of Oakland in 1957, and they have become the principal source of funding for Port projects. Nutter and his staff also devised innovative "mini-max" contracts for marine tenants. Annual payments fell within minimum and maximum limits, guaranteeing the Port revenue with which to service its bonds while providing a profit incentive for shippers.

By the time of his retirement in 1977, Nutter had overseen the development of most of the Port's container facilities. His handpicked successor, Walter A. Abernathy, was a former Oakland Chamber of Commerce executive who had joined the Port in 1964 as director of public relations, later serving as Nutter's assistant. In the same way that Dudley Frost, another non-engineer, had perpetuated the maritime policies of Arthur Abel, Abernathy carried forward Ben Nutter's commitment to containerization. During his twelve years as executive director, several new terminals would be opened.

Due to its global prominence, Oakland forged ties with many trading partners. The Port opened offices in Japan, Korea, Taiwan, Hong Kong, and Europe (as well as in Chicago, New York, and Washington). In 1970, the Port of Oakland began establishing "sister ports," now numbering more than a dozen around the world. Under a program instituted in 1978, dozens of officials from other nations, including the People's Republic of China, came to Oakland for training courses in port management. The program resulted in a definitive textbook, *Modern Marine Terminal Operations and Management*, which was published in 1983 by the Port of Oakland Maritime Division.

President Carter (center) on his 1980 tour of the Port of Oakland's container facilities. He is joined by Oakland Mayor Lionel J. Wilson and Port Executive Director Walter A. Abernathy.

51

An Overview of Oakland's Container Terminals

In 1999, the Port of Oakland had nine container terminals with a total of twenty berths and thirty cranes (including a dozen Post-Panamax cranes). All but one of these terminals were opened between 1962 and 1982. Three other facilities—the Outer Harbor's Bay Bridge and Burma Road Terminals, and the Inner Harbor's Ninth Avenue Terminal—are used primarily for break-bulk cargo and steel imports. In all, Oakland's marine terminals cover more than 600 acres and stretch over four miles of waterfront. The container terminals are discussed below.

In this 1969 view, Sea-Land's container yard fronts on the old Union Construction basin, adjoined by the Fourteenth Street Unit. A portion of the Oakland Army Base is visible in the foreground, on the site of the original plant of the Pacific Coast Engineering Company (Paceco). Sea-Land's first two Paceco cranes (insert) were the first container cranes on the Oakland waterfront.

Sea-Land Terminal (1962)

This Outer Harbor terminal is the Port of Oakland's oldest container facility. Negotiations with Sea-Land were initiated by Ben Nutter in 1961. On September 27, 1962, the containership *Elizabethport* inaugurated service between New Jersey and California. In 1966, Sea-Land switched from shipboard cranes to land-based cranes; the two Paceco A-frames installed that year were the first container cranes on Oakland's waterfront. The terminal, which originally covered about fourteen acres behind the Fourteenth Street Unit, underwent four major expansions in the 1960s as Sea-Land began supplying U.S. forces in Vietnam. By 1969, the forty-four-acre complex was the largest single-user container facility on the West Coast, with storage for 1,680 boxes. The terminal currently covers fifty-nine acres and includes three berths and four cranes. In terms of tonnage, Sea-Land remains the second largest ocean carrier (after American President Lines) at the Port of Oakland.

Seventh Street Terminal Area (1968/1971)

This Outer Harbor complex made Oakland a world-class port; it also made Ben Nutter's reputation. Undertaken at a time when containerization was in its infancy, Nutter launched the project prior to receiving commitments from tenants. The gamble paid off. When it was completed, Seventh Street ranked as the largest containerized shipping center on the Pacific Coast. As developed between 1965 and 1971, the facility comprised a 140-acre peninsula of filled land off the end of Seventh Street, with three separate terminals: Matson Terminal, Oakland Container Terminal, and Public Container Terminal. The current configuration includes two large terminals, Matson (sixty-five acres, three berths, three cranes) and Ben E. Nutter (fifty-eight acres, three berths, five cranes). A third terminal, TraPac, is located slightly inland on the site of the Albers Milling Company; opened in the 1990s, this last facility is discussed below under a separate heading.

The tideland site of the Seventh Street peninsula adjoined the Southern Pacific Mole, which reverted to Port ownership in 1960, at the end of SP's fifty-year franchise. When the Bay Area Rapid Transit District (BART) began construction of its interurban rail system, the Port granted an easement for a transbay tube under the mole. In exchange, BART agreed to clear the mole of buildings, construct a long dike in the bay, and fill the enclosure with excavated material from its projects. Groundbreaking ceremonies for the demolition phase took place on September 17, 1965. Several months later, work began on the 9,100-foot dike, and filling operations proceeded apace. The complex was designed and built by Kaiser Engineers of Oakland. The Port's later container terminals would be designed by its own expanded engineering staff.

The Seventh Street Terminal Area under construction, April 1968. The peninsular dike and fill extend out from the stub of the former Southern Pacific Mole. The long sides of the peninsula are parallel to existing shipping channels.

The Seventh Street complex as it appeared in the 1980s. The complex originally handled a limited amount of break-bulk cargo along with containerized cargo.

Dedication ceremonies at Seventh Street, September 12, 1968.

Matson Navigation Company signed the pivotal first lease in 1966, followed two years later by six Japanese lines. Showa and N.Y.K. Line agreed to share Matson's terminal. Japan Line, Kawasaki Kisen Kaisha ("K" Line), Mitsui O.S.K. Lines, and Yamashita-Shinnihon Steamship Company (Y.S. Line) formed a consortium to lease the adjoining Oakland Container Terminal. The opening of these two facilities, on September 12, 1968, coincided with the formal dedication of the Seventh Street complex. Ten days later, N.Y.K. inaugurated container trade between the United States and the Far East. By November, containerships from all six Japanese lines had completed maiden voyages to Oakland.

The Ben E. Nutter Terminal, at the peninsula's west end, was originally known as the Public Container Terminal, and later as the Marine Container Terminal. Financed primarily by federal grants and loans, the terminal opened in phases between 1969 and 1971; its formal dedication, on May 19, 1971, marked the completion of the Seventh Street Terminal Area. Open to all carriers, the facility's early users included Sweden's Johnson Line (later Johnson ScanStar), which inaugurated container service between Oakland and Europe, and the Pacific Australia Direct Line, which introduced "ro-ro" service (ships with ramps for vehicles and cargo carriers to "roll on" and "roll off"). Four Korean lines, including Hanjin and Hyundai, began calling at the terminal in the 1980s, making that nation Oakland's second largest trading partner after Japan. On June 17, 1998, with Nutter in attendance, the terminal was formally renamed in his honor.

N.Y.K. Line's Hakone Maru inaugurates container service between Japan and the United States at the Oakland Container Terminal, Seventh Street, September 23, 1968.

American President Lines Terminal (1969/1974)

Originally known as the Middle Harbor Container Terminal, this eighty-one-acre estuary complex is Oakland's largest single-user marine terminal. Situated near the foot of Adeline Street, the terminal began as two separate facilities. The Seatrain Terminal, at the east end of the complex, opened in 1969. Seatrain Lines purchased the property from Union Carbide and financed construction. Serving as a base of operations for the company's new California–Hawaii service, the facility grew to include two cranes and forty acres of storage yard. In 1971, the Port of Oakland acquired the terminal under a lease-back agreement. Three years later, the Port opened a new forty-acre, three-crane terminal on an adjacent site that had formed part of the Moore Dry Dock shipyard (which closed in 1961).

When it was dedicated in 1974, Middle Harbor Container Terminal combined both terminals in a four-berth, five-crane complex stretching over a half-mile of waterfront. The first tenant in the west section, United States Lines, remained until its bankruptcy in 1986. Maersk Line also used one of the berths prior to moving to the Outer Harbor. The terminal's principal tenant over the years has been American President Lines (APL), which moved its container operations and corporate headquarters from San Francisco to Oakland in the 1970s. Beginning in 1974, APL shared the east section of the terminal with Seatrain, which soon went out of business. Following the bankruptcy of United States Lines, APL also took over the west section of the complex. In 1987, the intermodal giant became the sole tenant of the renamed American President Lines Terminal, and soon passed Sea-Land as Oakland's tonnage leader. In 1996, the Global Alliance (which consists of American President Lines, Mitsui O.S.K. Lines, Orient Overseas Container Line, and Nedlloyd Lines) also began service at the terminal.

The Middle Harbor Container Terminal (now American President Lines Terminal) in the early 1980s. Naval Air Station Alameda lies across the estuary.

TransBay and Maersk Terminals (1977)

Following the opening of the Sea-Land and Seventh Street container terminals, the Port continued to use its older Outer Harbor facilities for break-bulk and bulk cargo. Between 1975 and 1981, the Seventh Street Unit, the Oil Pier, and the Fourteenth Street Unit were demolished and their sites redeveloped for container operations. The Outer Harbor Container Terminal occupied the site of the Seventh Street Unit and the Oil Pier complex. The terminal's south section (on the site of the Seventh Street Unit) was leased to the Japanese four-line consortium, which had outgrown the Oakland Container Terminal. Opened in January 1977, the two-berth, two-crane facility now covers twenty-nine acres; it was renamed the TransBay Container Terminal in 1986. The thirty-six-acre north section (on the Oil Pier site) opened in September 1977. The Danish-flag Maersk Line remains its principal user, and the one-berth, three-crane facility is now known as the Maersk Line Terminal.

Yusen Terminal (1981)

This forty-acre terminal, formerly known as the Outer Harbor Marine Container Terminal, occupies the site of the Port's Fourteenth Street Unit. Preferentially assigned to N.Y.K. and Neptune Orient Lines, the one-berth, one-crane facility is operated by Yusen Terminals. The adjacent Sea-Land yard occupies a portion of the Fourteenth Street Unit site as well.

Charles P. Howard Terminal (1982)

Adjoining Jack London Square on the Inner Harbor, the Charles P. Howard Terminal is the easternmost of the Port's container facilities. (The shallow depths of the Webster Street and Posey Tubes prevent deep-draft ships from going farther east on the estuary.) Covering fifty acres, the two-berth, four-crane terminal was built on the site of the Grove Street Terminal and the privately owned Howard Terminal, which the Port acquired in 1978. Demolition, dredging, filling, and construction extended over a three-year period. Dedicated on October 20, 1982, the facility was named in honor of the founder of the old Howard Terminal. Open

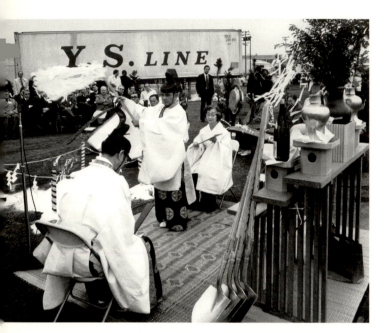

Shinto ceremony at the 1977 dedication of the Outer Harbor Container Terminal, now known as the TransBay Container Terminal.

The Outer Harbor in the late 1980s, showing the TransBay, Maersk, Yusen, and Sea-Land container terminals.

to all carriers, the terminal originally combined break-bulk and container operations. A remnant of the old Grove Street Pier transit shed stood until 1995, when the wharf and yard were enlarged and reconfigured solely for container use.

TraPac Terminal (1994)

Oakland's newest container facility, TraPac Terminal occupies the twenty-one-acre site of the Albers Milling Company plant. Vacated in 1985, the mill and grain elevators were demolished in 1988. Work began on the one-berth terminal in 1992. Formally dedicated on April 7, 1994, it is administered as part of the Seventh Street Terminal Area. TraPac is operated by Mitsui O.S.K. Lines through its subsidiary Trans Pacific Container Service Corporation. In 1996, ships of the Global Alliance also began calling here. The terminal's streamlined gate and office complex, computerized cargo-handling system, and two Post-Panamax cranes exemplify state-of-the-art container operations.

Charles P. Howard Terminal, 1993.

Gate and office complex, Trapac Terminal. Designed by the Oakland firm of Jordan Woodman Dobson, the terminal received a national design award from the American Institute of Architects.

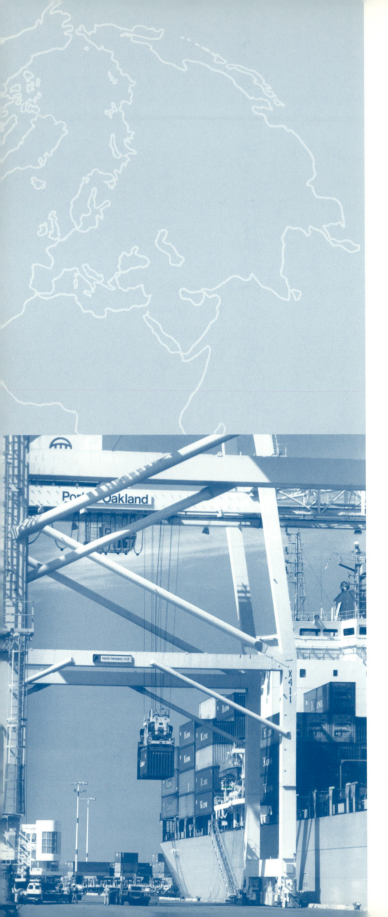

The Modern Intermodal Era

Since the 1970s, containerized shipping has continued to evolve in response to the global economy. Intermodalism is now characterized by ever-larger shipments of containers and increasingly integrated systems of cargo movement, and the role of Pacific Rim ports has been accentuated by generally strong Asian economies. A growing stream of goods flows back and forth across the Pacific Ocean and the North American continent, carried by the ships, trains, and trucks of new "multimodal" companies equipped to handle all phases of cargo movement.

The North American landbridge—the land-based transportation system linking ports on the West and East Coasts—has made the Panama Canal largely obsolete. The landbridge has become a cheaper and faster way to haul containers overland, utilizing modern double-stack trains with twice the carrying capacity of older trains. In port, the containers are picked up or delivered by huge Post-Panamax containerships which are too large to use the Panama Canal. Both modes of transport were pioneered in the 1980s by Oakland-based American President Companies, APL's multimodal parent company.

The major West Coast ports—Los Angeles, Long Beach, Oakland, Tacoma, Seattle, and Vancouver—have become competitive "gateways" serving the North American landbridge. In the 1980s, steps were taken to enhance Oakland's efficacy as a gateway. The Union Pacific (UP), which now controls the Western Pacific and Southern Pacific systems, inaugurated double-stack train service through California's Sierra mountain range in 1985. To assure continued containership access, Congress authorized a new dredging project in 1986, the first such project since the 1970s, when the Inner Harbor channel was deepened to thirty-five feet.

Along with channel widenings, the project called for deepening the Outer Harbor and Inner Harbor channels to forty-two feet. Delayed by environmental concerns, the dredging was completed in 1998.

Military base closures are making hundreds of acres of land available on

Double-stack train car.

58

Oakland's western waterfront for redevelopment. The 1999 reversion of the Navy's Fleet & Industrial Supply Center, Oakland, to Port ownership opened the way for new berths and an intermodal rail facility on the site. The reuse of the Oakland Army Base, slated to close in 2001, has yet to be decided.

The Port of Oakland is currently served by twenty major ocean carriers and more than a dozen smaller lines. Japan and Korea are Oakland's principal trading partners. Major imports include auto parts, computer equipment, clothing, and a wide range of processed and manufactured goods. Fruits, vegetables, and nuts remain the leading export items, followed by wastepaper, red meat and poultry, resins, chemicals, animal feed, raw cotton, logs and lumber, fertilizers, minerals, machinery, and cereal products.

Oakland retains its regional dominance, handling about 98 percent of the containerized cargo moving through the Bay Area, the nation's fifth largest metropolitan area, with a population approaching seven million. In terms of total containers handled (nearly 1.6 million TEUs in 1998), Oakland is third on the Pacific Coast after Los Angeles and Long Beach, fifth in the United States, and sixteenth in the world. Richmond, Northern California's other major port, specializes in bulk commodities such as petrochemicals, scrap metal, steel products, metal ores, gypsum products, and vegetable oils. The region is also served by smaller ports at Redwood City, Stockton, and Sacramento. The Port of San Francisco, once the undisputed leader, has lost most of its market share, and today deals primarily in cruise ships and waterfront tourism.

Intermodalism brought rapid evolution in the size and sophistication of containerships. Matson's Hawaiian Refiner *(left), a converted freighter capable of stowing a few dozen containers on its deck, sails past Jack London Square in 1959. APL's C-10-class* President Truman, *the world's first Post-Panamax containership, was designed to carry the equivalent of 4,300 twenty-foot containers on and below deck. The ship is shown here on its 1988 maiden voyage to Oakland's American President Lines Terminal.*

Vision

Vision 2000 and Channel Deepening

From its nineteenth-century origins as a rail center to its current prominence as an intermodal shipping center, Oakland has repeatedly demonstrated an openness to change, a willingness to adapt, and a capacity to innovate. In this spirit, the Vision 2000 Maritime Development Program addresses issues crucial to Oakland's future as a competitive port. The $700 million capital-improvement program, which has been made possible by the reversion of the Navy base to city ownership, is the largest maritime expansion in the Port's history.

Projects include a major reconstruction of existing facilities, the installation of a dozen new Post-Panamax cranes, and the development of a new four-berth terminal complex on the estuary (begun in 1999). At the center of the Vision 2000 area is the Joint Intermodal Terminal, a 340-acre rail facility planned for a portion of the Navy base site, inland from the new marine terminal complex. Consisting of a series of milelong tracks for loading and unloading containers, the terminal will be able to accommodate up to forty double-stack trains per day, making it one of the largest such facilities in the country. As a whole, the Vision 2000 program should assure the Port's stature as a world port into the next century.

The Port also proposes to deepen the federal shipping channels and most berths to a low-water depth of fifty feet in order to accommodate the newest generation of deep-draft containerships. The four-year project would involve the dredging and disposal of up to 12.9 million cubic yards of bottom sediments, and is expected to begin in 2000.

2000

Aviation

JULY 14, 1927
FIRST PRIVATE PLANE, CITY OF OAKLAND,
TAKES OFF FOR HONOLULU FROM
OAKLAND MUNICIPAL AIRPORT

Smith and Bronte head down the new 7,000-foot runway on Bay Farm Island—the start of
the second successful flight from North America to Hawaii.

CHAPTER FIVE   FROM KITTY HAWK TO BAY FARM ISLAND

viation has been a major activity at the Port of Oakland since the opening of the city's airport in 1927. Unlike the Port's maritime operations, which deal exclusively with cargo, aviation also involves passenger travel. Oakland International Airport remains one of Northern California's principal air terminals, accounting for a sixth of the Bay Area's airline passengers and half of the region's air cargo. Forty-five percent of current Port revenues are aviation related—an amount equivalent to the annual maritime earnings.

Aviation forms a recent chapter in the history of transport, dating back slightly more than 200 years. The invention of the airplane early in the twentieth century made air travel a practical reality. By the 1920s, rapid technical advances had ushered in the modern era of commercial aviation. It was during these years that Oakland, a city with a distinguished aeronautical heritage, established one of the country's busiest and best-known airports.

The Birth of Aviation: Balloons and Dirigibles

The age-old dream of human flight was first realized in France in the waning years of the eighteenth century. It was achieved with balloons—large bags of cloth or silk filled with hot air or hydrogen. Invented by the Montgolfier brothers, these lighter-than-air craft made their first ascensions at Paris and Versailles in 1783. During the nineteenth century, balloons were widely used in Europe and America for scientific research, military observation, and sheer adventure. They were an especially popular form of entertainment in the United States, where "aeronauts" toured the country taking passengers aloft.

Because free-floating balloons are at the mercy of the wind, they cannot be flown with precision. The solution was the dirigible, or airship—a streamlined gas bag equipped with rudder, motor, and propellers. The first practical models were flown in France in the late 1890s. By 1910, Count Zeppelin had established the world's first airline, deploying huge rigid-frame airships on scheduled routes across Germany.

Balloons and dirigibles appeared early in California skies. Aeronaut followed argonaut to the shores of San Francisco Bay, the state's population center after the Gold Rush. It was in Oakland, in 1853, that one of the first balloon ascensions

A crowd gathers at Fourteenth and Franklin Streets in downtown Oakland for the inaugural flight of the Oakland Aero Club's balloon, City of Oakland, *August 14, 1909. (Courtesy of the Oakland History Room, Oakland Public Library.)*

west of the Rockies occurred. A large crowd watched as the balloon slowly drifted over the hills to an eventual landing near Antioch. By the 1870s, balloon flights were being staged on a regular basis by amusement parks such as Woodward's Gardens in San Francisco, Blair's Park in Oakland, Shell Mound Park in present-day Emeryville, and the bayshore bathing resorts in Alameda.

"The balloon which ascended from Woodward's Gardens last Sunday, with Professor Martin and a San Francisco reporter as occupants, landed on the beach of Bay Farm Island," began a typical newspaper account of the period, published in the *Alameda Argus* in 1878. "It seems they narrowly escaped landing in the bay, and only avoided such a catastrophe by throwing overboard every movable article, including their lunch and scientific instruments."

Thomas Scott Baldwin's California Arrow *at Idora Park, Oakland, July 1904. (Courtesy of the Bancroft Library.)*

One of the country's best-known aeronauts was Thomas Scott Baldwin, a circus acrobat who turned to ballooning in the 1870s. His most daring feat took place in 1887, over Golden Gate Park, when he parachuted from his balloon at an altitude of 3,000 feet. Following a trip to Europe in 1903 to observe the new dirigibles, Baldwin designed and built the *California Arrow*, an airship powered by a custom-made Glenn Curtiss engine. On July 29, 1904, at Oakland's Idora Park, the *California Arrow* made the first successful airship flight in the United States.

Baldwin went on to build the country's first military dirigibles, and eventually the Navy would assemble a fleet of stately airships modeled after the Zeppelins. Yet dirigibles would ultimately prove to be a false start, a detour on the path to dependable air transport.

Advent of the Airplane

Throughout the nineteenth century, experimenters had grappled with the more difficult challenge of heavier-than-air flight. The problems were complex. Put simply, how do you lift a vehicle (without the aid of buoyant gas) and propel it through the air in a controlled manner? The lack of suitable engines until late in the century forced inventors to turn to gliding as a means of perfecting aircraft design and control.

The great pioneer in the theory and practice of heavier-than-air flight was the English baronet Sir George Cayley, whose observations of birds and kites led him to build the world's first glider by 1850. During the 1890s, Otto Lilienthal in Germany and Percy Pilcher in Scotland designed and flew sophisticated gliders; both men lost their lives in flying accidents. The momentum then shifted to the United States, where in a few short years the brothers Orville and Wilbur Wright made the quantum leap from gliding to powered flight.

The Wright brothers' first airplane (a modified biplane glider) flew at Kitty Hawk, North Carolina, on December 17, 1903. It was not until 1908, however, that the brothers began giving public exhibitions in the United States and Europe. By then, Glenn Curtiss of New York and several French designers had also built and flown aircraft. France reentered the aviation mainstream in 1909 with two historic events: Louis Bleriot's crossing of the English Channel in July of that year, and the world's first air meet, at Reims, in August. Of the thirty-eight airplanes entered in the meet—most of French design—twenty-three flew. Glenn Curtiss, the sole American competitor, set a world speed record of about forty-seven miles per hour.

Reims inspired a dozen major air meets in Europe and the United States over the following year. The first such event in the United States was held on Dominguez Ranch, south of downtown Los Angeles, in January 1910. The participants included several balloonists, two dirigibles, the Curtiss exhibition team, and French aviator Louis Paulhan, a veteran of Reims who piloted two Farman biplanes and two Bleriot monoplanes. Demonstrating superb skill and Gallic flair, Paulhan stole the show.

Kitty Hawk, December 17, 1903.

As the Dominguez Air Meet drew to a close, the Frenchman announced that he would travel north to give several more exhibitions. During three rainy days in late January, tens of thousands of Bay Area residents boarded special trains for Tanforan, a now-demolished racetrack near present-day San Francisco International Airport. There they observed Paulhan take off from the oval infield in his fragile machine, circle the track two times, climb to about 500 feet, fly out of sight, and dramatically return for a noiseless landing with the engine turned off.

The crowds watched the flights in rapt silence, followed by roars of approval. Spectators poured out of the stands and engulfed the aviator's tent, terrifying Paulhan and nearly causing a riot. Similar reactions were noted at many early air shows, when most people were witnessing an airplane for the first time. So it was that a French aviator and French aircraft introduced the Bay Area to the wonder of powered flight. The path from Kitty Hawk to San Francisco Bay passed through Paris—not a straight line, but then history rarely is.

Pioneer Oakland aviator Peter Allinio at Sunset Field, Alameda, 1912. (Courtesy of the Bancroft Library.)

Wings over the Bay

The year 1910 was a pivotal one for American aviation. For the first time, airplanes were seen by large numbers of people in many parts of the country. In the Bay Area, Paulhan's exhibition was followed by two other air shows, and by the end of the year several small airfields were in use. In January 1911, Tanforan, renamed Selfridge Field, would serve as the site of the region's first large air meet—an event made famous by Eugene Ely's unprecedented "carrier" landing onto the deck of a modified Navy cruiser.

Oakland and Alameda were among Northern California's earliest and most active flying centers. Alameda hosted the Bay Area's first competitive air meet on an April weekend in 1910. Staged on the grounds of the old Neptune Gardens resort at the foot of Webster Street, the show featured balloon ascensions, gliding contests, and the inaugural Northern California appearance of a Curtiss biplane. Piloted by Marin County sportsman Frank Johnson ("the millionaire aviator"), the plane made several skimming flights along the shore, crashing once in the bay.

The Christofferson Flying Boat Aermaide *on the Oakland waterfront, 1914. (Courtesy of the Oakland Museum of California.)*

Later that year, a few aviators began pitching tents and parking their aircraft next to a little-used racetrack on the Alameda marsh east of Webster Street, not far from the estuary waterfront. It was there, in 1912, that two exhibition fliers, Frank Bryant and Roy Francis, established the Sunset School of Aviation, one of the first flying schools in the Bay Area. During the few years it remained in operation, Sunset Field presented a lively scene.

The Chinese-American aviator Tom Gunn, who taught at the Sunset School, made demonstration flights in Alameda in 1912 for military attachés of China's first president, Sun Yat-sen. Later that year, Gunn left the United States to oversee flight instruction and aircraft construction in the Chinese republic.

The most accomplished student to earn his wings at Sunset Field was Silas Christofferson, a twenty-one-year-old automobile mechanic from Oregon. In 1912, the novice became an overnight sensation when he took off from

Tom Gunn

Cooke at the controls of the Diamond.

Mayor Mott presenting the Chamber of Commerce trophy to Cooke at Lakeside Park, January 1912.

Weldon B. Cooke

the roof of a Portland hotel and flew across the Columbia River to Vancouver, Washington. Silas and his brother Harry returned to the Bay Area later that year, where they became widely known as pilots, instructors, and aircraft designers.

For a brief period in 1914, the two-passenger Christofferson Flying Boat served as an air ferry on a scheduled route between Oakland and San Francisco—in essence, one of the first airlines in the United States. When their airplane factory was moved from San Francisco to Oakland in 1915, the brothers established a new flying school on the Alameda marsh west of Webster Street; in 1916, they shifted their operations to Redwood City.

Oakland's pioneer aviators congregated in Elmhurst, a lightly populated section of East Oakland in the vicinity of San Leandro Bay. The Oakland Motordrome, located on East Fourteenth Street near Seventy-third Avenue, served as Elmhurst's first airfield. The first flier to base his operations at the motordrome, early in 1911, was Fung Joe Guey, a resident of Oakland's Chinatown who may have flown an airplane of his own design as early as 1909. Guey left California in the spring of 1911 to become one of China's first exhibition fliers.

Oakland's best-known aviator, Weldon B. Cooke, taught himself to fly in the *Diamond*, a Curtiss-type biplane designed and built in 1910 by L. B. Maupin and Bernard Lanteri of Pittsburg, California. Hired as their pilot, Cooke began making flights out of Elmhurst in the fall of 1911. In October he was credited with being the first man to fly over Oakland; in December he crossed the bay to circle high above Mt. Tamalpais. In order to qualify for the 1912 Dominguez Air Meet, Cooke earned a prestigious license from the Aero Club of America. He performed

70

his flying tests before a large crowd at Oakland's Lakeside Park, where he was presented with an honorary silver trophy, and later won a first prize at Dominguez. Cooke went on to tour professionally, also serving as the first pilot on the Christofferson air ferry.

In February 1912, the recently closed Emeryville Race Track (renamed the Oakland Aviation Field) became the venue for the East Bay's first big air show. Billed as an "aerial three ring circus, a thrill every second," the Oakland Aviation Meet featured races and stunts by local fliers and nationally known figures such as Blanche Scott, whose flights there were probably the first made by a woman in California. The star of the show was the celebrated San Francisco daredevil Lincoln Beachey; according to the *Alameda Times-Star*, his Curtiss biplane "dropped like a twisting rocket, careened around the track in imitation of a runaway bronco, tumbled and tossed like a ship at sea, brushed the tops of hooded autos, and cut wild rings around a lofty flagpole." Beachey would return to the Oakland Aviation Field in 1914, during a national tour, to race a car around the oval. The following year the racetrack was demolished.

Many of the Bay Area's aviation pioneers ultimately lost their lives in flying accidents: Ely, in 1911; Guey, in 1912; Cooke, in 1914; Beachey, in 1915; Silas Christofferson, in 1916. The death tolls mounted, wherever men and women dared to fly.

(Top) Lincoln Beachey soars over the racetrack grandstand at the Oakland Aviation Meet in Emeryville, February 1912. (Courtesy of Louis Stein and the Emeryville Historical Society.)

Lincoln Beachey racing Barney Oldfield at Emeryville, 1914. (Courtesy of the Bancroft Library.)

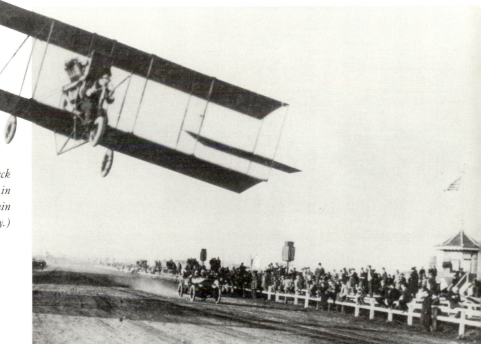

The Air Age

Aviation came of age during World War I, when aircraft proliferated in a wide variety of specialized types, from fighters to multiengine bombers. Warplanes could now climb above 20,000 feet and attain speeds up to 150 miles per hour. In sheer numbers, the transformation was staggering. When the United States declared war in 1917, the nation's combined air forces (Army, Navy, and Marine Corps) consisted of ninety-nine airplanes and eighty-three pilots. By the time of the Armistice in 1918, the United States had over 10,000 military aircraft and an equal number of pilots and mechanics.

Curtiss, the leading manufacturer during the war, had produced in excess of 4,000 aircraft; most of these were JN-4 trainers, popularly known as "Jennies." Purchased by the War Department at $5,000 apiece, a surplus Jenny could be had after the war for as little as $400. These sturdy biplanes provided wings for many ex-military fliers who toured the country as barnstormers, performing stunts and selling rides.

Technical advances forged during the war made long-distance flights possible for the first time. In 1919, a mere ten years after Bleriot flew the English Channel, the Atlantic was crossed by warplanes. The following year, the Post Office Department inaugurated transcontinental airmail service, flying its own fleet of planes between New York and San Francisco. In 1923, the Army Air Service completed the first nonstop coast-to-coast flight—lasting twenty-seven hours— followed in 1924 by a grueling six-month circumnavigation of the globe.

Aerial view of Durant Field, Oakland, looking southwest toward San Leandro Bay, circa 1920. (Courtesy of the Bancroft Library.)

The Bay Area remained one of the country's aviation centers. Crissy Field, the western terminus for transcontinental airmail, served as the region's principal air terminal. Placed in operation in 1921 by the Army Air Service, this up-to-date facility occupied a bayshore site at the San Francisco Presidio. Crissy Field was the Bay Area's first military air base and the first airfield in the region to have permanent hangars. Its clay-surfaced runway extended 3,300 feet.

Oakland's Durant Field, opened in 1919, was the East Bay's most important new airfield. Situated south of East Fourteenth Street between Seventy-seventh and Eighty-fourth Avenues, the field was developed by R. Clifford Durant, an Oakland automobile manufacturer and amateur pilot, as a base of operations for his Durant Aircraft Corporation (which maintained a fleet of Jennies for charter use). With its dirt strip and wooden hangars, Durant Field recalled the pioneer facilities of the previous decade. Its heyday was brief; by 1924, factories covered much of the site. For Oakland, a modern and permanent airport had become a pressing need.

• Durant Field

Bay Farm Island •

Curtiss Jennies lined up to perform at the Flying Derby air show, Durant Field, May 1920. (Courtesy of the Oakland Museum of California.)

The hangars at Durant Field. (Courtesy of the Oakland Museum of California.)

73

Establishing Oakland Municipal Airport

Commercial aviation became big business in the latter half of the 1920s as airlines began carrying mail and passengers on scheduled routes. Dozens of airports sprang up across the country during these years. In the Bay Area, the trendsetters were the municipal airports at Oakland and San Francisco, both dedicated in 1927, and still in operation. Two commercial airfields in Alameda, Alameda Airport (1928) and San Francisco Bay Airdrome (1930), lasted only a decade.

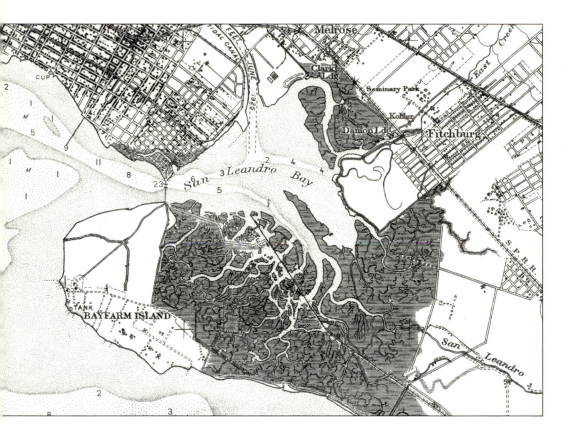

Bay Farm Island in the mid-1920s. The actual "island" consisted of a 230-acre upland (lower left) adjoined by hundreds of acres of marshland. (San Francisco Bay, Southern Part: West Coast, California, U.S. Coast and Geodetic Survey, 1926. Courtesy of the Map Room, Doe Library, University of California, Berkeley.)

The federal government played a pivotal role fostering commercial aviation in the United States. Beginning in 1925, airmail contracts were put out to bid to private carriers, providing fledgling airlines with vital economic support (in the same way that mail contracts had subsidized early steamship lines). Federal legislation also set strict new standards for rating airports, regulating routes, inspecting aircraft, and licensing pilots.

Oakland Municipal Airport grew out of this national surge in air commerce. The impetus for the project came from the Aviation Committee of the Oakland Chamber of Commerce, which mounted a campaign for a municipal airport in 1925. Late that year, based on the committee's recommendation, the city government secured an option for a large marshland tract on Bay Farm Island, a sparsely settled shoreline area in Oakland's southeast corner.

First settled in the 1850s, Bay Farm Island had remained an agricultural backwater in the metropolitan East Bay. The "island" was actually a marshy peninsula bordered on the south and west by San Francisco Bay and on the north by the San Leandro Bay inlet. The peninsula's west end, forming part of the city of Alameda, contained farmland, a residential subdivision, and a soon-to-open municipal golf course. The eastern section, within Oakland, was marshland.

74

The bayshore site was ideal for airport purposes. Located only six miles from downtown Oakland, yet sufficiently isolated to allay noise and safety concerns, the terrain was unobstructed by trees or tall structures. Visibility was enhanced by over-water approaches and minimal low-level fog. The site could accommodate long runways, with ample acreage for future growth.

In November 1926, shortly before the option was to expire, the Oakland City Council gave its initial approval to purchase the 680-acre tract for $625,000. In January 1927, following final passage of the ordinance, responsibility for the airport's development and operation was transferred to the newly established Port of Oakland. At its very first meeting, in February 1927, the permanent Board of Port Commissioners formally assumed control of the facility.

Final acquisition of the airport property proved complicated. To begin with, the legality of the Port's jurisdiction over the airport was uncertain; the city ordinance establishing the Port of Oakland made no mention of aviation. A related question concerned the use of Port funds to acquire the airport property; the municipal bonds approved by voters in 1925 were ostensibly limited to maritime projects. Several months would pass before these issues were settled in the Port's favor.

The City Council had agreed to purchase the Bay Farm Island property in a series of payments extending over ten years, and a $65,000 down payment was made in January 1927. To maintain control of its own operations, the Board of Port Commissioners decided to acquire the site outright. The balance of $560,000 was drawn from the 1925 bond fund, and title to the property passed to the Port of Oakland in August 1927. Two land acquisitions over the following year enlarged the site to 850 acres.

During this same period San Francisco established its own municipal airport. After studying a number of sites (including Bay Farm Island), the city government had secured a lease from the Mills Estate for a 150-acre bayshore tract in San Bruno. Situated near the old Tanforan airfield, the site lay about twelve miles south of downtown San Francisco. Mills Field was formally dedicated on May 7, 1927, and hurriedly placed in operation early the following month. The rudimentary facilities included a hangar and several short runways.

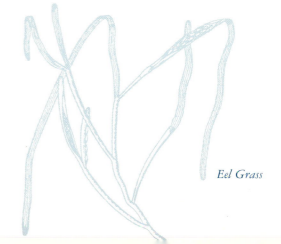

Eel Grass

A Flying Start

As Mills Field opened for business, Port of Oakland crews were frantically at work on a 7,020-foot runway—the first construction project at the new airport. The crews used mule-drawn graders to complete the job in a little over three weeks. The shoreline airstrip, unusually long for its day, was rushed to completion at the request of the Army Air Service, which had announced that in June 1927 an Army plane would attempt to cross the Pacific from California to Hawaii.

The flight would rival in importance Lindbergh's recent solo crossing of the Atlantic. Navy seaplanes based at Crissy Field had tried—and failed—to reach Hawaii in 1925. The Army was confident that its big Fokker C-2 transport would

The Bird of Paradise *taking off from Bay Farm Island, June 28, 1927.*

Hegenberger and Maitland.

succeed. Because the fuel-heavy monoplane required an extremely long runway, Oakland was chosen as the point of departure in place of Crissy Field.

On June 28, 1927, Bay Farm Island experienced its first traffic jam. Thousands of spectators jostled with newspaper reporters and newsreel cameras as the *Bird of Paradise* lumbered down the runway with Lt. Lester Maitland and copilot Lt. Albert Hegenberger at the controls. The next day the plane set down at Oahu's Wheeler Field, logging 25 hours, 50 minutes, in the first successful aerial crossing of the Pacific Ocean.

Two other aviators—former airmail pilot Ernest Smith and his navigator, Emory Bronte—attempted to race the Army plane but were forced back due to a broken windscreen. Two weeks later, on the morning of July 14, Smith and Bronte took off from Oakland in their Travel Air monoplane *City of Oakland*. They ended their flight on Molokai, besting the Army's time by fourteen minutes and becoming the first civilian fliers to cross the Pacific.

Bronte and Smith.

The Bird of Paradise *and* City of Oakland *on the new runway, June 1927.*

Start of the Dole Race, August 16, 1927.

Then came the Dole Race. Sponsored by Hawaiian pineapple magnate James D. Dole, who announced the race in late May 1927, the competition offered a $25,000 first prize and a $10,000 second prize to the first two planes "to cross from the North American continent to Honolulu in a nonstop flight." The race was scheduled to begin no earlier than August 12, 1927, the anniversary of Hawaii's annexation to the United States. Although the choice of a takeoff point was left open, Bay Farm Island soon emerged as the favored field among the contestants. In addition to being closer to the islands than most other airfields on the West Coast, Oakland was already well known for its runway and its two recent transoceanic flights.

Art Goebel, winner of the Dole Race, poses with the Woolaroc. One of only two planes in the race equipped with a radio, the Woolaroc also benefited from the expert navigation of Naval aviator William Davis.

As it turned out, the Dole Race was a disaster. Three people died in crashes en route to Oakland; seven others were lost at sea. Of the original fifteen entrants, only eight airplanes lined up for the start on August 16 (four days late due to last-minute preparations). Two planes crashed attempting to take off; a third was disqualified; three others vanished without a trace, including the *Miss Doran*, which carried as a passenger a young schoolteacher named Mildred Doran. Only two airplanes finished the race. The winner, at 26 hours, 17 minutes, was Art Goebel of Santa Monica, piloting a Travel Air monoplane identical to the one flown the month before by Smith and Bronte.

Second-place finisher Martin Jensen and the Aloha.

Pilot John Augy Pedlar (above), his passenger, Mildred Doran (left), and his navigator were lost at sea during the Dole Race. Their airplane, the Miss Doran, *is shown taking off from Bay Farm Island. (Courtesy of the Oakland Museum of California.)*

Martin Jensen   winner of 2nd Place

Dedicating the Airport

The inspiration for the Dole Race was Charles Lindbergh—the twenty-four-year-old former airmail pilot and barnstormer who, on May 20–21, 1927, had flown a California-built Ryan monoplane, the *Spirit of St. Louis*, from New York to Paris. He instantly became the most celebrated aviator of his time as well as a potent catalyst and spokesman for commercial aviation. Americans adulated their new hero, and he coaxed them into the sky.

Charles A. Lindbergh at the dedication of Oakland Municipal Airport, September 17, 1927.

The man himself, piloting his famous plane, visited the Bay Area in September 1927. Sponsored by the Guggenheim Fund for the Promotion of Aeronautics, Lindbergh was nearing the end of a 22,350-mile tour of the United States. The three-month odyssey included visits to all 48 states. The aviator would stop in 82 towns and cities, attend 69 banquets, and deliver 147 speeches extolling the virtues of air transport and stressing the need for a national network of airports.

By the time he reached the Bay Area, two months into the tour, the reclusive flier had lost twenty-five pounds and was in a state verging on nervous exhaustion. He flew south from Portland (where he had dedicated the city's new airport) one month after the Dole Race, touching down at Mills Field in the early afternoon. Paraded up Market Street in San Francisco, he was feted that evening with a banquet at the Palace Hotel.

The following morning, Lindbergh took off from Mills Field and spent an hour flying around the bay before making his final approach to Oakland. On the marshland below was a sight by now familiar to him: automobiles parked in long rows by a dirt airstrip, spectators massed around a makeshift speaker's platform. The *Spirit of St. Louis* touched down on Bay Farm Island at 11:30 a.m.

Roscoe D. Jones, president of the Board of Port Commissioners, proclaimed that Oakland was "honored by having this great airport dedicated by this splendid young American who is the idol of all our people and who is a torch lighting the airways of the world." Lindbergh gave a short speech in which he praised the airport as "the best field I have ever seen" and spoke briefly about the future of aviation. He then unveiled a bronze plaque honoring Maitland and Hegenberger. By 12:30 p.m. he was gone, bound for Sacramento.

As the *Spirit of St. Louis* droned into the distance, tens of thousands of East Bay residents headed for home, elated at having seen and heard the country's most famous man. The Port commissioners were probably a little dazed themselves. An astonishing series of events had thrust their airport onto the world stage before the first hangar was even built. It was time to get down to business.

Lindbergh on a later visit to Oakland, accompanied by Airport Superintendant Guy Turner.

81

OAKLAND MUNICIPAL AIRPORT
TOTAL AREA - 890 ACRES

Clyde
SUNDERLAND

Oakland Municipal Airport in 1940.

he transoceanic flights of 1927 brought instant fame to Oakland's fledgling airport. That memorable summer came to a close with Lindbergh's dedication of the field, which then consisted of one long runway and little else. Within two years, a modern and sophisticated facility would take shape on the Bay Farm Island marsh.

Prior to World War II, Oakland ranked as Northern California's leading commercial airport, handling the greatest number of airline passengers while serving as a regional center for federal aviation officials and military reservists. During the war, when commercial flights ceased, Oakland lost its lead to San Francisco. Oakland Municipal Airport would gain new prominence in the postwar era as the headquarters for a succession of charter airlines. Largely intact, it remains one of the nation's most historic aviation sites.

Building the Airport

Oakland Municipal Airport was planned and built with remarkable speed. Under the supervision of Gustave Hegardt and Arthur Abel, Port of Oakland engineers initiated design studies early in 1927. Construction began late that spring and was completed by the fall of 1929. As in the case of the Port's maritime facilities, all site improvements (with the exception of the original runway) were carried out by private contractors. This intensive first phase of development, completed at a cost of $1.5 million, resulted in Northern California's largest and best-equipped airport.

The Port of Oakland relied on the expert advice of military and federal officials in all matters relating to the airport's development and management. Major Delos C. Emmons, commanding officer of Crissy Field, recommended the siting for the original runway. Other officials who worked closely with the Port included Assistant Secretary of War for Aeronautics F. Trubee Davison, Assistant Secretary of Commerce for Aeronautics William P. McCracken, and Department of Commerce Director of Aeronautics Clarence M. Young.

"The utility of Oakland Municipal Airport . . . is not limited to its being the takeoff point for spectacular flights. Over a period of years, it has been developed to the point where it is today the most completely equipped airport in the West, and the only air terminal on the Pacific Coast which has met all of the United States Department of Commerce requirements for the safe transport of passengers."

1932 Oakland Tribune Year Book

As originally built, Oakland Municipal Airport covered about a third of the Port's property on Bay Farm Island (which totaled 890 acres by 1940). The principal structures—five hangars, an administration building, a restaurant, and a hotel—were grouped in a row at the north edge of the field, adjoined by a frontage road, parking lot, railroad spur, and boat dock. Runways and taxiways occupied the remainder of the site.

The first construction project was the long runway rushed to completion in June 1927 by Port of Oakland crews. The first outside contracts, for two hangars and an administration building, were awarded the following month; construction began in August, shortly after the Dole Race. Guy M. Turner, the foreman on the runway job, was appointed in July as the airport's first superintendent—a position he was to hold for twenty-five years. A Navy veteran long associated with military aviation, Turner would provide on-site supervision of all early construction projects in addition to his day-to-day duties overseeing operations.

The airport in the winter of 1927–28, looking west across Bay Farm Island. Two hangars have been built, and the grass-covered airfield still shows the pattern of recently installed drainage conduits.

Hangar No. 2 soon after it opened. (Courtesy of the Oakland Museum of California.)

The most prominent structures at the original airport are five gable-roofed hangars erected between 1927 and 1929. All are of steel-frame construction, with cladding of corrugated sheet steel. Tall rolling doors at the ends provide access for aircraft; shed-roofed bays along the sides contain workshops and offices. The foundations, floors, and abutting aprons are concrete.

Hangars No. 1 and No. 2, each measuring 90 by 200 feet, were placed in operation in December 1927. Much of the steel for these two buildings came from the old quay-wall transit shed, measuring 90 by 400 feet, which was dismantled during construction of the Grove Street Pier. Hangar No. 3 (1928), 120 by 200 feet, and Hangar No. 4 (1928–29), 122 by 300 feet, were considered the nation's largest nonmilitary hangars at the time of their completion. The most elaborate structure in the group, Hangar No. 5 (1929), has the same hangar dimensions as No. 4 but is enhanced with a Spanish-styled office wing along its street front.

Interior of Hangar No. 5 in 1929. (Courtesy of the Oakland Museum of California.)

Hangar No. 5 in 1998.

85

The administration building in 1927, soon after completion.

Oakland Airport Inn

OAKLAND, CALIFORNIA

◆

HOUSE RULES

Your conformance to the following house rules is prompted only for your own comfort and convenience which we know you will appreciate. You understand that it is the desire of the management to afford you the utmost of comfort while here as our guest.

Guests in overalls, or without coat, are not permitted in dining room or hotel lounge.

Radios to be turned off not later than 10:30 P. M.

Boisterous conversation in entertaining is prohibited in rooms, halls or restaurant at all times.

Breakage of furniture or other equipment, through action of guest, must be paid for.

The management will not permit the storage or use of intoxicating beverages in rooms or premises.

Rates, weekly or monthly, to be paid in advance.

Being a gentleman, we know you will conduct yourself as such among gentlemen.

The lobby of the Oakland Airport Inn as it appeared in 1935. Note the bas-relief dirigible on the mantle of the fireplace (left).

The administration building, which opened on October 31, 1927, was the airport's first permanent structure. Classical in design, with a temple front and recessed portico, it housed the superintendent's office, mail and radio rooms, pilot's sleeping quarters, and a passenger lounge. In 1928, the building was doubled in size to accommodate the offices of the U.S. Weather Bureau. Its current utilitarian appearance dates from a 1939 remodeling.

A hotel and restaurant with stuccoed exteriors occupied the east end of the row; both were operated as concessions by the Interstate Company. The restaurant (no longer standing) opened for business in the summer of 1928. The two-story Oakland Airport Inn—widely advertised as the country's first airport hotel—was formally dedicated on July 30, 1929. Prior to its 1940s remodeling as a terminal and offices, the building had a delightful lobby with an aeronautical motif featuring images of airplanes and dirigibles woven into the curtains and embossed on the mantle of a large fireplace.

As the airport buildings assumed shape, work proceeded on basic site improvements. Extensive filling and grading were required, shoreline dikes needed strengthening, and entirely new water, sewer, and drainage systems had to be installed. Drainage, critical to the marshland site, was provided by two main conduits and numerous laterals laid in rock-filled trenches. Most new construction after 1929 dealt with extending and resurfacing the field, originally planted in grass. As planes grew heavier, it became necessary to upgrade the runways and taxiways with crushed rock, and finally with asphalt and concrete.

Convention visitors stroll past the restaurant in the summer of 1932.

The field side of the restaurant and hotel, early 1930s.

From the beginning, Oakland Municipal Airport was one of the best-equipped fields in the United States for night flying. The lighting system, as planned by the Department of Commerce, included rotating beacons, floodlights, and neon-lit markers. Throughout the night, a green auxiliary beacon flashed the letters "OK" in Morse code, signifying "Oakland Municipal Airport" to night fliers.

Access by land was improved by a new thoroughfare running south from East Oakland along the east side of San Leandro Bay. Opened in 1930, the roadway was named in honor of Army pilot Albert Hegenberger. (The shoreline road connecting the airport to Alameda and San Leandro had been renamed Maitland Drive in 1927.) There was even an attempt to create a water route by cutting a channel through the marsh to San Leandro Bay. In 1929, speedboats began carrying passengers between the airport dock and downtown San Francisco, but the service never caught on. The channel would later see use as a seaplane basin.

Hangars No. 4 and No. 5 form a backdrop to seaplanes in the Airport Channel, 1930.

DEPARTMENT OF COMMERCE
AIRWAYS RADIO STATION

DEPARTMENT OF COMMER
RADIO BEACON

8336'

TOTAL AIRPORT AREA
850 ACRES

3000'

UNITED AIR LINES
BOEING AIR TRANSPORT
PACIFIC AIR TRANSPORT
BOEING SCHOOL OF AERONAUTICS

U.S. NRAB
Squadron 14

SOUTHERN PACIFIC RAILROAD

AIRPORT INDUSTRIAL AREA
135 ACRES

SEAPLANE
RAMP

AIRPORT CHANNEL

PREVAILING WINDS

ILLUMINATED CIRCLE

HANGAR No. 5

HANGAR No. 4

HANGAR No. 3

HANGAR No. 2

HANGAR No. 1

AIRPORT DOCK

ADMINISTRATION BUIL
Airport Superintenden
Department of Commer
U.S. Weather Bureau
U.S. Post Office
First Aid Station
Flight Surgeon
Public Telephones
Telegraph

7200'

5000'

MAJOR OPERATIONS AREA
260 ACRES

AIRPORT INN
AND RESTAURANT

1800'

NEON LIGHTED
WIND TEE

COMPASS
TABLE

OAKLAND

© SUNDERLAND STUDIOS

OAKLAND MUNICIPAL AIRPORT
U.S. GOVERNMENT RATING A1A

The airport in 1930.

In this 1930 aerial view, the airport is shown in relation to other Port of Oakland facilities. The privately operated Air Ferries Terminals on the Oakland and San Francisco waterfronts provided transbay taxi service with amphibious planes.

Early Airlines

The first scheduled airlines at Oakland Municipal Airport were Boeing Air Transport, which began service on December 15, 1927, and Pacific Air Transport, a Boeing subsidiary that commenced operations on February 1, 1928. Boeing held the mail contract between the Bay Area and Chicago; Pacific flew the coast mail route between San Diego and Seattle. By 1930, both companies were divisions of United Air Lines, the country's largest commercial carrier.

As the western terminus of the main transcontinental air route and the central division point for transports heading up and down the coast, Oakland was one of the most important airports in the country. With increasing frequency, Boeing, Pacific, and United airliners carried passengers and cargo on each of the mail routes in and out of Oakland—to Chicago/New York, Portland/Seattle, and Los Angeles/San Diego.

Boeing and Pacific (and later United) based their operations at Oakland, leasing Hangars No. 1 and No. 2 prior to occupying Hangars No. 4 and No. 5 in 1929. Hangar No. 5 became the airport's busiest building, serving as the passenger terminal and operations center for Oakland's major airlines. The airport's first control tower was built on the field side of the hangar in 1937. The upper floor of the office wing housed the prestigious Boeing School of Aeronautics, a Boeing affiliate that trained pilots and mechanics for various airlines.

Boeing 40 mail and passenger plane, Pacific Air Transport, late 1920s. (Courtesy of the Oakland History Room, Oakland Public Library.)

Boeing 80 night flight.

Twelve-passenger Boeing 80, Boeing Air Transport, 1928. (Courtesy of the Oakland Museum of California. Oakland Tribune Collection. Gift of the Alameda Newspaper Group.)

A busy day at the airport in 1930. The large monoplane is a Fokker transport operated by Western Air Express. The administration building, restaurant, and hotel form a row beyond Hangar No. 1.

The earliest type of airliner to fly out of Oakland was the Boeing 40, a two-passenger biplane manufactured by the parent company of the Boeing and Pacific lines. The Boeing 80, a trimotor biplane carrying twelve passengers, began flying in the summer of 1928, and an eighteen-passenger version went into service in the fall of 1929. The cruising speed of these early transports averaged 100 miles per hour, which meant that a flight to Chicago (with stops en route) took around twenty hours. With the introduction of the advanced Boeing 247 in 1933, followed by sleek DC-3 Mainliners in 1936, United was able to reduce travel time by up to one-half on its transcontinental and coast routes.

While United remained Oakland's flagship carrier, smaller airlines also provided passenger and cargo service. Mutual Inland, Century Pacific, Maddux, and Varney linked Oakland to numerous cities in the region. Western Air Express inaugurated its "model airway" between Oakland and Los Angeles in 1928, using powerful Fokker transports. Over the following decade Western's successor, Transcontinental & Western Air (TWA), would continue to provide daily service to Los Angeles and points east.

United Air Lines DC-3 Mainliner by the control tower at Hangar No. 5, 1940.

Mainliner cabin.

Passenger volumes at Oakland grew rapidly during the 1930s, when the airport was rated as one of the nation's busiest. From a mere 4,000 airline passengers in 1929, the annual total increased to nearly 70,000 by 1939, peaking at 91,000 in 1940. These figures far outpaced the region's other airports.

For most people air travel remained a novelty, and visitors were a common sight on weekends and holidays. To accommodate the crowds, the Port opened a spectator's plaza in 1928 between Hangars No. 2 and No. 3. A small building was added in 1933 to exhibit the *Diamond* biplane flown by Weldon Cooke—one of two historic aircraft donated to the Port that year (the other was displayed in Hangar No. 3). The plaza was closed to the public in the 1940s, and both biplanes ended up in the Smithsonian.

In this staged view from 1933, two 1910 biplanes flank one of United's new Boeing 247 airliners, dramatizing aviation's rapid development in the early twentieth century. The biplanes were donated to the Port of Oakland and placed on display at the airport.

On the apron.

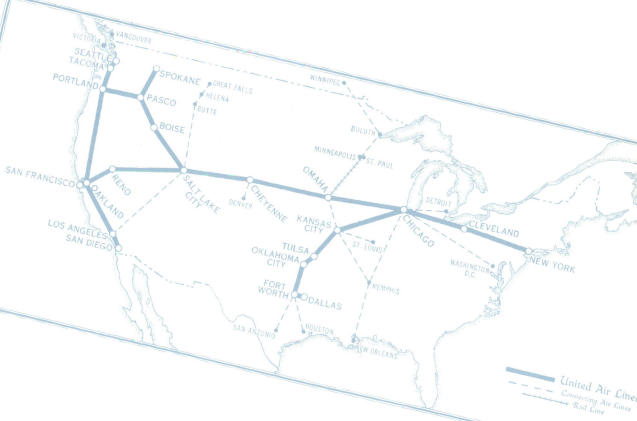

93

Other Operations

Airlines were not the only activity at Oakland Municipal Airport. Small commercial operators like Fillmore, Duck, and Moreau offered a variety of "air services," from flying lessons to sightseeing and charter trips. Vendors sold aircraft, made repairs, and supplied parts. In 1940, the Port erected a building on the east half of the public plaza for lease to Pacific Airmotive, the airport's leading supply-and-repair company.

Oakland also played an important role as a regional headquarters for federal agencies related to aeronautics. The first to locate there, in 1928, was the U.S. Weather Bureau. In 1929, the Department of Commerce began broadcasting periodic weather reports to aircraft from a radio station at the Alameda end of Bay Farm Island. The Department of Commerce also maintained a radio range beacon near the airport for transmitting directional signals. Federal licensing and inspecting over a wide region were supervised out of the Oakland office.

Military aviation established an early and lasting presence. In the summer of 1928, Oakland was chosen as the site for a Naval Reserve Air Base, one of three such installations (with Long Beach and Seattle) in the western United States. Starting with two antiquated trainers, USNR Squadron 14 grew to include ten planes by 1933, when it was joined by Marine Corps Reserve Squadron 8. A separate Army Air Corps Reserve Unit with two squadrons was established in 1936. At first, the military leased hangar and tarmac space from the Port; this would all change during the war.

In the midst of these day-to-day activities, spectacular events continued to make headlines. On May 31, 1928, Sir Charles Kingsford-Smith and a three-man crew departed Oakland in the trimotored *Southern Cross*, arriving in Brisbane seven days later, by way of Hawaii and Fiji, to complete the first transpacific flight from North America to Australia. He then proceeded to circle the globe; the circumnavigation, made in stages and delayed by a crash,

Douglas Gullwing bomber used for airmail flights in 1934, when the Army briefly carried the mail for the Post Office Department.

Naval Reserve planes at Oakland, 1934.

Pacific Airmotive Building nearing completion in the summer of 1940.

94

ended at Oakland on July 4, 1930. Four years later, Kingsford-Smith reprised his first feat by flying east from Australia to Oakland.

Of the many famous fliers associated with the airport, none was more compelling than Amelia Earhart. Her connection with Oakland began in 1931, when she crossed the country in a hybrid airplane/helicopter called an autogiro. Following a 1932 solo flight over the Atlantic, Earhart set her sights on the Pacific. On January 11–12, 1935, piloting a Lockheed Vega, she logged 18 hours, 15 minutes, in the

Crew of the Southern Cross *in 1928 (left to right): Capt. Harry Lyon, Jr., navigator; Capt. Charles T. P. Ulm, copilot; Capt. Charles Kingsford-Smith, pilot; James Warner, radioman. (Courtesy of the Oakland History Room, Oakland Public Library.)*

first solo crossing from Hawaii to North America, touching down at Oakland before an adoring crowd. Bay Farm Island also served as the point of departure for Earhart's ill-fated round-the-world flight in 1937, which ended with her disappearance over the Pacific.

Other well-known aviators came to Oakland to perform in shows. Thousands of spectators turned out in 1938 for the Pacific International Air Races, a three-day extravaganza showcasing the speed of Earl Ortman and the aerobatics of Tex Rankin and Paul Mantz. Historic flights and elaborate air shows highlighted the airport's prominence in the prewar period.

Amelia Earhart poses for a newsreel camera in front of her twin-engine Lockheed Electra, Oakland Municipal Airport, spring of 1937. She is flanked by technical adviser Paul Mantz (left) and navigators Harry Manning and Fred Noonan (right).

Paul Mantz at the Pacific International Air Races, 1938.

Regional Developments

For the Bay Area at large, these were years of robust growth for commercial and military aviation. In addition to Oakland, the region was served by three modern airports and three newly commissioned air bases.

The military bases were the result of national-defense planning and intense local lobbying. In 1936, the Army completed construction of Hamilton Field in Marin County, replacing Crissy Field at the San Francisco Presidio. The Navy's Moffett Field, established in Sunnyvale in 1933, began as a dirigible base and later served as a conventional airfield. Naval Air Station (NAS) Alameda, commissioned in 1940, had as its primary mission the overhaul of aircraft for the Pacific Fleet. Built on reclaimed tidelands south of the Alameda Mole, NAS Alameda formed the first link in a chain of Navy and Army bases stretching across the western waterfronts of Oakland and Alameda.

Airship Akron *at Moffett Field, early 1930s.*

In the commercial sector, San Francisco made steady advances. Mills Field, renamed San Francisco Airport in 1931, grew over the course of the decade to encompass 1,100 acres. Runways were improved and a new terminal building was dedicated. Passenger volumes increased as United, TWA, and other airlines offered more frequent flights. The airport's resurgence culminated with United's decision, late in 1940, to move its administrative and maintenance operations from Oakland to San Francisco, presaging the end of Oakland's regional dominance.

Two smaller airports were situated in the East Bay city of Alameda, adjoining Oakland. Alameda Airport opened in 1928 on a narrow strip of filled land bordering the Alameda Mole, some two miles off Alameda's western shore. Developed with private capital on land leased from the city, and later acquired by the Curtiss-Wright Corporation, the facilities included a two-story administration building and a seaplane basin doubling as a yacht harbor.

San Francisco Airport during the 1931 National Air Tour. (Courtesy of the Oakland Museum of California. Oakland Tribune Collection. Gift of the Alameda Newspaper Group.)

Alameda Airport had limited success at first. Its principal carrier, Maddux Air Lines, a Curtiss-Wright subsidiary flying between the Bay Area and Los Angeles, soon discontinued service. In 1935, Pan American Airways (PAA) subleased the

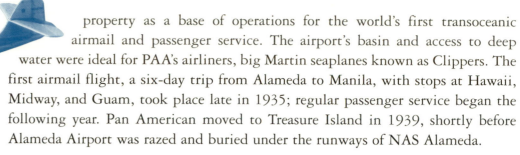

property as a base of operations for the world's first transoceanic airmail and passenger service. The airport's basin and access to deep water were ideal for PAA's airliners, big Martin seaplanes known as Clippers. The first airmail flight, a six-day trip from Alameda to Manila, with stops at Hawaii, Midway, and Guam, took place late in 1935; regular passenger service began the following year. Pan American moved to Treasure Island in 1939, shortly before Alameda Airport was razed and buried under the runways of NAS Alameda.

Alameda's other commercial field was the San Francisco Bay Airdrome. Covering 250 acres of reclaimed marshland west of Webster Street (on the site of the Christofferson brothers' flying school), the airport was dedicated in the summer of 1930. It had runways paved with oyster shells, lights for night flying, and an enormous hangar measuring 120 by 600 feet. Western Air Express, one of the principal investors in the new airport, shifted its operations from Oakland, only to discontinue service in 1931. Increasing air traffic from NAS Alameda forced the airdrome's closure in 1941.

Alameda Airport in 1933, looking north to Oakland Outer Harbor. The China Clipper *(insert) was one of three Pan American transpacific airliners based at the airport after 1935.*

The big hangar at the San Francisco Bay Airdrome, viewed from Webster Street, 1932.

Contemporary view of Hangars No. 7 and No. 8, built at NAS Oakland during World War II.

World War II

Air power played a decisive role in the war in the Pacific, with the Bay Area serving as a vital staging area for planes and supplies. One of the busiest facilities was NAS Alameda, which supplied Pacific Fleet carriers with new and refurbished aircraft. The Bay Area's two principal airports also came under military control. At Oakland, commercial operations were curtailed late in 1941, ceasing altogether by 1943; at San Francisco, domestic airlines continued to offer flights, giving that airport an enormous advantage in the postwar boom in air travel.

The war years at Oakland Municipal Airport were marked by round-the-clock military activity. The Navy carried out a dual mission of training and transport, while the Army Air Corps processed thousands of fighters and bombers. Oakland Naval Reserve Air Base, recommissioned late in 1941, occupied totally new facilities at the west end of the field. Instructors provided training in Stearman N2S biplanes prior to 1943, when the base was taken over by the Naval Air Transport Service and renamed Naval Air Station (NAS) Oakland. By the end of the war, NAS Oakland covered sixty-five acres and included three large hangars in addition to warehouses, barracks, and other facilities.

Blimp from NAS Oakland over NAS Alameda, late 1940s.

Looking east over Oakland Municipal Airport, circa 1946. NAS Oakland (foreground) borders the Airport Channel.

The high volume of wartime air traffic prompted the Army and Navy to collaborate on the construction of a new runway on filled land south of the old airfield. Completed in 1945, the 6,200-foot airstrip brought the total number of runways to three.

Oakland Municipal Airport would retain a military flavor long after the war. NAS Oakland, which resumed its original function as a Naval Reserve Air Base in 1946, remained in operation for another fifteen years. Throughout this period, the Port of Oakland cosponsored annual air shows with the Navy (and for several years after the war, with the Army). The Navy base reverted to the Port in the early 1960s, when the facility was closed and its squadrons transferred to NAS Alameda.

Airliners parked in front of the administration building, 1952.

Army Airborne Show, November 1945—the first postwar air show at Oakland Municipal Airport.

The Postwar Era

By war's end in 1945, Oakland had relinquished its role as the region's leading commercial airport to San Francisco. United and Pan American (which left Treasure Island in 1944) maintained operating bases at San Francisco, as did two other wartime acquisitions, TWA and Western. Soon eight major airlines served the airport. In addition to handling most of the region's domestic air travel, San Francisco cornered the market on international flights, which became an everyday reality in the postwar era.

San Francisco Airport tallied one million annual passengers shortly after the war, when "International" was added to its name. Now covering more than 2,100 acres, the field included a six-story terminal complex and expanded runways for the new generation of ocean-hopping airliners—big four-engine transports like the DC-6, DC-7, Lockheed Constellation, and Boeing Stratocruiser, which carried as many as 100 passengers at cruising speeds exceeding 300 miles per hour. The decade culminated with the inauguration of jetliner service in 1959; that year, the airport handled over four million passengers.

TWA Constellation at Oakland, 1950s.

When commercial flights resumed at Oakland in the years 1945–46, passenger volumes lagged far behind those of San Francisco. Major airlines such as United, TWA, American, and Western scheduled so few flights that the airport's prewar peak of 91,000 annual passengers would not be equaled until the early 1950s. Most destinations were cities in California and the western United States, with limited service to the East Coast and Hawaii, and no scheduled international flights. The Board of Port Commissioners filed numerous complaints with the Civil Aeronautics Board (CAB) concerning inadequate service and unfair practices, but the situation would not begin to improve until the advent of jetliner service in the 1960s.

The administration building in the 1950s.

101

OAKLAND MUNICIPAL AIRPORT

Enhanced photograph of the airport in the late 1940s. Runway 27-L (left) and Naval Air Station Oakland (upper right) were wartime additions.

Charter Airlines

Oakland made do in other ways, primarily in the burgeoning field of nonscheduled carriers. These airlines—also known as charter, contract, or supplemental carriers—flourished after the war by using cheap surplus aircraft to haul passengers and freight under military and commercial contracts. For several decades Oakland would serve as a base of operations for a succession of major charter airlines, led by Transocean Air Lines and World Airways.

Transocean, founded in Oakland in 1946 by Orvis M. Nelson, became the world's largest nonscheduled carrier with its fleet of surplus C-54 (DC-4) transports. In addition to airlift contracts with the military, Transocean pioneered the concept of low-cost charters to Europe and Hawaii. The airline trained thousands of pilots and flight attendants through a subsidiary, the Taloa Academy of Aeronautics. Another subsidiary, the Aircraft Maintenance & Engineering Company (AMECO), overhauled Air Force transports and provided foreign airlines with DC-4s converted from military use.

Transocean charter, 1949. (Courtesy of the Bancroft Library.)

Hangar No. 6, contemporary view.

Transocean was Oakland Airport's principal tenant in the late 1940s and 1950s. The airline and its subsidiaries leased a number of facilities. Hangar No. 5 became the company's headquarters, and the old Airport Inn was remodeled to serve as the airline's "International Terminal." Hangar No. 6—the only major construction project at the airport during this period—was erected by the Port of Oakland in 1958 expressly for lease to AMECO. Overextended and saddled with debt, Transocean filed for bankruptcy in 1960.

Transocean's successor in spirit and deed was World Airways. Founded in New Jersey in 1948 and acquired two years later by Edward J. Daly, World Airways moved its headquarters to Oakland in 1956, eventually taking over many of Transocean's facilities. By the mid-1960s, it was the world's leading charter carrier. In the 1980s the airline moved its base of operations back to the East Coast, marking the end of an era at Oakland.

The departure of World Airways coincided with the biggest surge in scheduled passenger service in Oakland's history. The resurgence began twenty years earlier, when an entirely new airport was developed south of the old field. It is to this modern facility that we now turn.

C-124 Globemaster at Hangar No. 6, 1958. This hangar, one of the world's largest at the time of its completion, was used by Transocean subsidiary AMECO to refurbish military aircraft.

The new airport (South Field) soon after its completion in 1962.

CHAPTER SEVEN   OAKLAND INTERNATIONAL AIRPORT

T*he 1962 dedication of a new runway and terminal inaugurated the jet age at Oakland International Airport. Seven years under construction, the new airport was built on reclaimed tidelands in the bay, south of the old field. Passenger volumes surged in the 1960s and again in the 1980s, when a second terminal opened. Oakland continued to be known during these years as a center of the charter-airline industry; since then, scheduled cargo carriers have become a significant source of jobs and revenues. The original airport, now known as North Field, remains in operation as a general aviation and air-cargo facility.*

The region's three international airports—Oakland, San Francisco, and San Jose—are all in the midst of major expansion programs. If these plans come to fruition, the Bay Area will accommodate eighty million airline passengers by the year 2010—twenty million more than it does today. Oakland International Airport, which currently handles 15 percent of the Bay Area's airline passengers and 48 percent of air cargo, is poised to maintain its share of the metropolitan market into the twenty-first century.

Airport Expansion

The Port of Oakland put forth its first proposals for airport expansion on the eve of World War II. During the war, with commercial operations at a standstill, the Port focused its energies on planning and land acquisition. The Airport Master Plan of 1944 envisioned a $10 million reconstruction of the existing field by extending the runways into the bay. New facilities were to include a five-story passenger terminal and a maritime-industrial complex on San Leandro Bay which would be closely linked to the airport.

This ambitious plan remained Port policy for nearly a decade. Executive Director Dudley Frost, newly appointed in 1952, placed a high priority on airport development, and in 1953 Oakland voters approved $10 million in general-obligation bonds for the expansion. Issued in 1955, these were the first voter-approved bonds for Port purposes since 1925. They also proved to be the last; in 1957, the Port instituted its current practice of using revenue bonds to finance its projects.

Airport expansion as envisioned in the 1940s.

The passenger terminal under construction, 1961.

The Board of Port Commissioners requested an updated study from Knappen, Tibbetts, Abbett, McCarthy (KTAM), a New York engineering firm specializing in airport planning and development. KTAM's report called for an entirely new complex on filled tidelands south of the existing field. Hegenberger Road would be extended around the east end of the old field to provide access to the new passenger terminal. One long runway would form the airport's south edge, providing unobstructed over-water approaches for jet airliners; provision was also made for a second, parallel runway as the need arose. This "offshore" plan was approved in March 1954 by the Port commissioners, who jubilantly voted at the same meeting to change the name of Oakland Municipal Airport to Metropolitan Oakland International Airport (commonly known as Oakland International Airport).

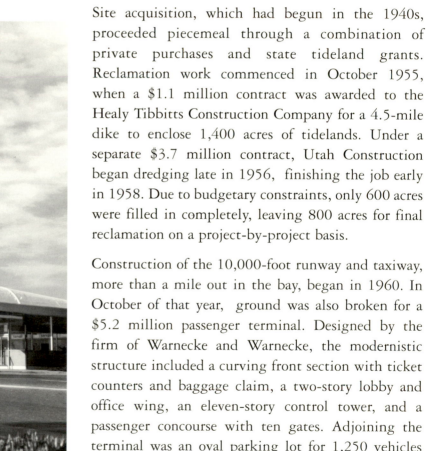

The terminal in the 1960s.

Site acquisition, which had begun in the 1940s, proceeded piecemeal through a combination of private purchases and state tideland grants. Reclamation work commenced in October 1955, when a $1.1 million contract was awarded to the Healy Tibbitts Construction Company for a 4.5-mile dike to enclose 1,400 acres of tidelands. Under a separate $3.7 million contract, Utah Construction began dredging late in 1956, finishing the job early in 1958. Due to budgetary constraints, only 600 acres were filled in completely, leaving 800 acres for final reclamation on a project-by-project basis.

Construction of the 10,000-foot runway and taxiway, more than a mile out in the bay, began in 1960. In October of that year, ground was also broken for a $5.2 million passenger terminal. Designed by the firm of Warnecke and Warnecke, the modernistic structure included a curving front section with ticket counters and baggage claim, a two-story lobby and office wing, an eleven-story control tower, and a passenger concourse with ten gates. Adjoining the terminal was an oval parking lot for 1,250 vehicles (later enlarged to 7,000 spaces).

The new airport was completed at a cost of $20 million, with most of the additional $10 million provided by federal grants. Operations commenced gradually over the spring and summer of 1962. The first jet to use the new runway, in May, was a private plane piloted by the well-known aviator Jacqueline Cochrane. The control tower was placed in operation in July.

The formal dedication of Metropolitan Oakland International Airport extended over the weekend of September 15–16, 1962. Attended by more than 100,000 people, the event was scheduled to coincide with the airport's thirty-fifth anniversary. The festivities began with the arrival of a Pan American cargo plane from Thailand carrying an elephant for the Oakland Zoo. Stunt pilots Paul Mantz and Frank Tallman entertained the crowds in vintage aircraft while jets from NAS Alameda screamed overhead. Guests of honor included Lester Maitland, Albert Hegenberger, Ernest Smith, Art Goebel, and other transpacific pioneers. Chief Justice Earl Warren, who had attended the original airport dedication in 1927 as Alameda County District Attorney, unveiled the dedicatory plaque.

The airport emerges from the bay, 1958.

Dedication ceremonies, September 1962.

The Jet Age

The advent of dependable jet transports in the late 1950s revolutionized the airline industry. The jetliners had seating capacities exceeding 150 and cruising speeds above 500 miles per hour. Faster and larger planes meant more passengers on more frequent flights; this greater efficiency brought down ticket prices, making air travel accessible to the public at large. As passenger volumes soared in the 1960s, the nation's airports experienced unprecedented growth. In the Bay Area, the total number of airline passengers handled by San Francisco, Oakland, and San Jose more than tripled over the course of the decade, from 5 million to 17.5 million.

On June 1, 1963—four years after jets began flying out of San Francisco—TWA inaugurated scheduled jetliner service at Oakland International Airport, placing Convair 880s on its Chicago and New York flights. One week later, United Airlines commenced jet operations between Oakland and Los Angeles. American Airlines put Boeing 707s on its Oakland routes in 1964.

Jets gave rise to the first real surge in passenger traffic at Oakland since the 1930s. The airport handled 426,000 passengers in 1963, a 36 percent increase over 1962. The milestone of a million passengers was passed in 1966, and by the end of the decade Oakland was handling two million passengers a year. Most of

this traffic was generated by short-haul carriers flying up and down the state. In 1965, Pacific Southwest Airlines (PSA) and Western Airlines introduced cut-rate fares on their Oakland–Los Angeles commuter flights. By the end of the year, Western had converted its aging DC-6 fleet to Boeing 720s, and PSA had replaced its prop-driven Electras with 727s.

Despite its name, Oakland International Airport handled few scheduled international flights, though Oakland-based charter airlines frequently flew to other countries. To accommodate the growing number of charter flights, a two-gate International

Lobby of the passenger terminal in the 1960s.

Arrivals wing for customs and immigration was added to the terminal in the early 1970s. For a brief period, Oakland also provided transbay helicopter and hovercraft service for East Bay residents booked on overseas flights out of San Francisco.

Scheduled passenger volumes rose only slightly during the 1970s, peaking at 2.9 million in 1979. This slow rise was a reflection of sluggish growth in the airline industry at large, due to recession, inflation, and rising fuel prices. Yet Oakland's problems were also local in nature. Residential development on the west end of Bay Farm Island had raised new concerns about noise and safety. In 1975, the city of Alameda and Harbor Bay Isle Associates sued the Port, halting all construction at the airport; the Port's countersuit froze the planned Harbor Bay Isle development.

The 1976 settlement agreement restricted new Alameda residences to areas outside the airport's Noise Impact Zone (demarcated by "noise contour lines"). In turn, the Port agreed to prepare an Environmental Impact Report for its Airport Master Plan, and to establish a preferential-runway-use program as a means of curtailing westbound departures from North Field. Subsequent residential growth on Bay Farm Island has contributed to continued strained relations between the Port of Oakland and the city of Alameda.

The airport was also hampered by inadequate airline service, a chronic problem since World War II. In 1977, the Board of Port Commissioners filed yet another petition with the Civil Aeronautics Board. Supported by seven airlines, the Port won a stunning victory in 1978 when the CAB voted to allow carriers "unlimited entry" into the Oakland market. The ruling was intended as an experiment—allowing market forces to replace federal intervention as a means of determining effective service. In fact, it was the case that triggered airline deregulation, ushering in the modern era of air travel in the United States.

Bay Farm Island in the late 1940s, looking east to Oakland Municipal Airport. Approximately 350 people then resided within Alameda city limits (foreground).

Bay Farm Island in the late 1990s, looking east to Oakland International Airport. The parallel runways of the old airport (upper center in both pictures) provide a common point of reference. Farms have given way to subdivisions and townhouses, and the tidelands have been replaced by the Harbor Bay Isle development. Current estimates place Bay Farm Island's residential population at 13,000. (Courtesy of Pacific Aerial Surveys.)

When it opened in 1973, the World Air Center was one of the nation's largest nonmilitary hangars.

Twilight of the Charters

Throughout these years, Oakland International Airport continued to serve as a global center for the charter airlines—nonscheduled, supplemental carriers that transport passengers and cargo under contract. By 1970, four of world's top five nongovernmental charter airlines—World, Trans International, Saturn, and Universal—were headquartered at Oakland.

By the 1960s, World Airways had established itself as the world's largest privately owned supplemental carrier. In 1967, with most of its fleet converted to jets, the airline executed a forty-year lease for a giant new hangar and office building on a sixty-acre site near the terminal. Designed for the new generation of jumbo jets, the World Air Center enclosed 180,000 square feet of hangar space and could accommodate four 747s or six DC-10s at a time. The federally funded $11 million building (formally named in honor of East Bay Congressman George P. Miller) was dedicated on May 7, 1973. Several days later, World Airways inaugurated 747 service at Oakland International Airport.

Boeing 747C on display at the dedication of the World Air Center.

Trans International Airlines (TIA), the world's second largest contract carrier, moved its headquarters to Oakland in 1963. The owner of the very first DC-8 off the production line, TIA instituted jet operations at the new airport several months earlier than the scheduled airlines. Following its 1976 merger with Saturn Airways, TIA overtook World Airways as the largest private charter airline. It was acquired soon after by the Transamerica Corporation and renamed Transamerica Airlines.

The golden age of the supplementals ended in the 1980s. Stiff competition from deregulated airlines and scheduled cargo carriers, as well as shrinking military contracts and rising operating costs, contributed to the decline. Transamerica Airlines ceased operating in the mid-1980s, about the time World Airways moved its headquarters to the East Coast, where it has remained in business on a reduced scale. Since 1988, the former World Air Center has been used by United Airlines as a maintenance center for its jumbo jets.

TIA charter flight, 1970. This planeload of servicemen returning from Vietnam on leave was greeted by actor Jimmy Stewart and the Oakland Raiderettes.

TIA headquarters, North Field, 1967.

San Francisco International Airport. (Courtesy of SFO.)

San Jose International Airport. (Courtesy of SJC.)

Bay Area Boom in Air Travel

The demise of the charter airlines coincided with the biggest surge in scheduled passenger service in Bay Area history. Fueled by a strong economy and rapid population growth in the nation's fifth largest metropolitan area, as well as cheap fares following deregulation, airline travel has soared over the past two decades. In the mid-1980s, the region's three major airports served about thirty million passengers a year. By 1998, the total approached sixty million.

San Francisco International Airport (SFO)—the fifth busiest airport in the U.S. and seventh busiest in the world—continues to handle most of the Bay Area's passenger travel. The airport's eighty gates were served by more than fifty airlines in 1998; that year's total of thirty-nine million passengers included 95 percent of the Bay Area's international travelers. Equipped with four runways and three terminals, the 2,340-acre complex is undergoing a major expansion that includes a new International Terminal and a BART extension. If approved by regulatory agencies, three new runways may be added.

San Jose International Airport (SJC) is a relative newcomer. Though the South Bay city had several small airfields prior to World War II, with limited service via Oakland, it was not until 1949 that San Jose Municipal Airport opened on a 1,050-acre site near the downtown. The airport's growth has been spurred by rapid urbanization associated with the Silicon Valley boom; today San Jose ranks as the Bay Area's most populous city. Jetliner service began at the airport's new terminal in 1966, leading to a doubling of passenger volumes over the next two years. Renamed San Jose International Airport in 1984, and enhanced with a second terminal in 1990, SJC is currently served by a dozen airlines, primarily short-haul carriers. In 1998, the airport's thirty gates handled 10.5 million passengers.

Metropolitan Oakland International Airport (OAK) has also experienced dramatic growth over the past two decades. The 2,580-acre facility entered the 1980s prepared for change. The first significant project involved the replacement of the terminal's ground-level gates with ten new gates arrayed in an upper-level concourse equipped with jetway bridges.

The new passenger concourse at Terminal 1, opened in 1980.

Metropolitan Oakland International Airport.

Terminal 2 under construction (above). Baggage-claim pavilion (below).

Upon completion of this project, planning began for a new seven-gate terminal. Two years under construction, Terminal 2 (named for Oakland Mayor Lionel J. Wilson) formally opened on May 17, 1985. Designed by Ratcliff Architects, the space-frame structure was praised by the *San Francisco Chronicle* architecture critic Allan Temko as "just about the finest facility of its kind in the country." The terminal was built expressly for PSA and Air California commuter flights; in 1988, operations were taken over by Southwest Airlines, currently Oakland's leading carrier. Recent improvements to the terminal complex include a new baggage-claim wing, a glass-enclosed passageway linking the two terminals, and the addition of three new gates.

Passenger volumes at Oakland have tripled since the early 1980s. Much of this traffic has been generated by high-volume, short-haul carriers like Southwest flying up and down the coast. In 1998, the airport's twenty-two gates handled 9.2 million passengers. In 2000, domestic scheduled service was offered by seven airlines—Alaska, Aloha, American, America West, Delta, Southwest, and United—with scheduled international flights provided by Martinair Holland, Taesa, Mexicana, City Bird, and Corsair.

Terminal 2 (foreground) soon after completion.

Air Cargo

In recent years, the Port of Oakland has promoted the development of freight operations as a complement to passenger services. Air cargo is a labor-intensive activity that generates jobs as well as revenues, and the Port has chosen to promote air cargo both for its local employment opportunities and its profitability. Today, Oakland International Airport ranks among the nation's top fifteen airports for air cargo. Prior to the 1970s, most freight was hauled by supplemental carriers based at North Field. The first cargo facility at the new field opened in the late 1960s, west of the passenger terminal. At that time, 200 acres were also set aside in the nearby Business Park for development as an air-cargo distribution center.

Oakland's leading cargo carriers are Federal Express (FedEx) and United Parcel Service (UPS). The first to arrive, in 1975, was UPS, which established its regional trucking center at the Business Park. In conjuction with this facility, UPS planned to develop a regional hub for its jets at the airport, but environmental litigation halted filling operations at the site (UPS eventually built its hub at Ontario, in Southern California). Federal Express, the world's largest package carrier, came to Oakland in 1979, six years after the company was founded. Oakland soon became FedEx's West Coast hub, one of the carrier's six U.S. distribution centers. FedEx's Oakland sort facility, opened in 1988 on a twenty-seven-acre site west of Terminal 1, handles approximately 300,000 packages per night.

The airport's cargo volumes (primarily small packages) have risen sharply since the mid-1980s, from 125 million pounds in 1984 to nearly 1.5 billion pounds in 1998. (The 1998 cargo totals for San Francisco and San Jose were, respectively, 1.3 billion pounds and 250 million pounds.) In addition to FedEx and UPS, scheduled cargo carriers at Oakland in 2000 included Airborne Express, Emery Worldwide, and Kitty Hawk.

The airport's air-cargo facility (foreground) in the 1980s. Federal Express and United Parcel Service jets are parked on the ramp.

FedEx's regional sort facility at Oakland opened in 1988.

North Field

Oakland is one of the few major airports in the United States to have made the transition to commercial jet operations without replacing its original facilities. The old airport, known since 1962 as North Field, is now used primarily for general aviation—private aircraft, corporate jets, flight schools, aerial advertisers, and related businesses. North Field is one of the country's busiest airports for general aviation. Indeed, in terms of total number of takeoffs and landings—two-thirds of them at North Field—Oakland ranks as the ninth busiest airport in the world.

Port of Oakland Executive Director Walter A. Abernathy looks on as Oakland Mayor Lionel J. Wilson and President Thomas L. Berkley of the Board of Port Commissioners formally open North Field's first Executive Terminal, July 1980.

The Federal Aviation Administration opened a new regional facility at North Field in 1966, and in 1972 a new control tower was placed in operation at the south edge of the field. An executive terminal was opened in 1980 on the flight line, followed by a second, larger terminal in the late 1980s. Roads, parking lots, and utility systems have been largely rebuilt. The most substantial recent development is Chevron's $8.3-million corporate hangar, which opened in 1995.

North Field's principal fixed-base operator is KaiserAir. The company provides an entire range of services for corporate and private aircraft, from fueling to maintenance, and it runs both executive terminals. The Sierra Academy of Aeronautics, headquartered in the old Airport Inn since the 1970s, trains technicians, mechanics, pilots, and dispatchers for the airlines. National Airmotive overhauls and repairs engines for commercial and military clients. Dozens of other businesses at the airport offer products and services relating to general aviation.

Air cargo and aircraft maintenance are also important activities at North Field. Cargo facilities, which are concentrated in the former Navy base at the west end of the field, include a U.S. Postal Service airmail distribution center. Hangar No. 6, formerly operated by Transocean and World as a maintenance center, has served since 1989 as a systemwide maintenance facility for Alaska Airlines.

The new Executive Terminal.

Chevron's corporate hangar at North Field.

119

Redolent with the past, North Field remains a mecca for aviation buffs. Most of the original facilities are still standing, and in 1980 the field was designated an Oakland City Landmark. Historic flights continue to be made. In 1967, Ann Pellegreno commemorated the thirtieth anniversary of Amelia Earhart's attempted round-the-world flight, starting and ending her successful circumnavigation (in a vintage airplane) at North Field. Linda Finch replicated this feat in 1997. Aviation history is also celebrated at the Western Aerospace Museum, a nonprofit institution opened at North Field in 1986. Among the memorabilia and aircraft on display is a twin-engine Lockheed Electra, sister ship of the plane in which Earhart disappeared.

Ann Pellegreno

Western Aerospace Museum

Looking to the Future

If the 1980s and 1990s marked the end of military aviation in the Bay Area—these years witnessed the closure of Hamilton Field, Moffett Field, and Naval Air Station Alameda—for commercial aviation it has been a period of unprecedented growth. Current development plans of the Bay Area's three international airports project a regional total of eighty million annual passengers by the year 2010.

The Port of Oakland's Airport Development Program calls for a variety of projects to meet near-term needs and to provide flexibility for long-term planning. Unveiled in 1993, the $900 million capital-improvement program envisions an increase in the airport's annual capacity to 13.8 million passengers and two billion pounds of air cargo by 2010. The centerpiece of the program is an expanded terminal complex with thirty-four gates, served by a two-tier roadway system and a large parking structure. Other projects include a BART connector, improved access to I-880, and a major addition to FedEx's sort facility. In all, the development program, the most ambitious since the opening of South Field, should assure Oakland's place in the regional market for decades to come.

Artist's conception of the terminal expansion proposed in the Airport Development Program.

2010

121

The Waterfront & The Community

The redevelopment of Jack London Square nears completion, 1990. The newly opened seven-story Port of Oakland Building (left foreground) is adjoined by a seven-level parking structure. Other new buildings, including the Waterfront Plaza Hotel, extend along the estuary waterfront to the central plaza.

he Port of Oakland's Commercial Real Estate Division manages over 1,000 acres of land and water along nineteen miles of the city's waterfront. Most of this acreage has been conveyed to the Port through the State Tidelands Trust. Over 6.4 million square feet of commercial and industrial space are contained within the shoreline Port Area, including offices, retail stores, restaurants, and hotels, accounting for nearly 10 percent of the Port's annual revenues.

Compared to the Port's maritime and aviation operations, commercial land development is a recent activity. The first major ventures, Jack London Square and the Oakland Airport Business Park, were undertaken after World War II. The Port has also developed marina complexes and shoreline parks, situated for the most part on former industrial sites on the estuary. Nearly $30 million in capital improvements are now planned or underway.

Jack London Square

The best known and most central of the Port's commercial developments, Jack London Square extends six blocks along the waterfront in the vicinity of Broadway. Initially developed in the 1950s, the area has largely been rebuilt since the 1980s. The mix of restaurants, retail stores, offices, hotels, and entertainment venues attracts over six million visitors a year, providing employment for thousands of Bay Area residents.

Antecedents

Jack London Square occupies the site of earliest Oakland. It was here, where Broadway meets the estuary, that Horace Carpentier built the town's first wharf and established the first regular ferry service between the East Bay and San Francisco. It was here that the downtown began its block-by-block migration up Broadway. And it was here that the city's working waterfront was at its most vibrant, bristling with wharves, coal bunkers, lumberyards, planing mills, foundries, and factories. Sailing ships frequented the docks west of the Webster Street Bridge; freight trains rumbled down the center of First Street; teamsters threaded their wagons through gangs of stevedores and seafarers. This was the milieu that nourished the imagination of Jack London.

Oakland Lumber Company, First Street and Broadway, 1894. A ferry is berthed at the "Creek Route" slip at the foot of Broadway. (Courtesy of the Oakland History Room, Oakland Public Library.)

The Port of Oakland can also trace its origins to this section of the waterfront. The city's first municipally owned wharf opened at Webster and Franklin Streets in the 1870s, and early in the century other city-owned port facilities were built in the area. For many years the Port of Oakland maintained its headquarters at the nearby Grove Street Pier. It seems fitting that this stretch of shoreline should serve as the site of the Port's earliest commercial venture.

The Board of Port Commissioners made its first foray into waterfront tourism in the 1930s, when the old municipal wharf was replaced with two modern facilities—the Inland Waterways Terminal (1931) at Webster Street, and Fishermen's Pier (1936) at the foot of Franklin. Inspired by the example of Fisherman's Wharf in San Francisco, Fishermen's Pier included berths for commercial fishing boats, outlets for wholesale and retail seafood, and a two-level restaurant later known as the Oakland Sea Food Grotto. Two other restaurants, the Bow & Bell and the short-lived Planter's Dock, opened in the 1940s on sites leased from the Port at the foot of Broadway. These early establishments made little provision for pedestrians or parking, fitting rather uncomfortably into their industrial setting on the working waterfront.

The restaurant at Fishermen's Pier, soon after its opening in 1936 (left), and the Bow & Bell as it appeared in the 1950s (above).

126

Establishing Jack London Square

The Port commissioners broached the idea of an expanded retail district for the area during the summer of 1948. The catalyst was Fishermen's Pier, then in need of refurbishing. In September of that year, the Board discussed "the desirability of developing a plan for the area between Webster Street and Broadway on the waterfront for restaurants and concessions similar to the development which has taken place in San Francisco." Two years would pass, however, before plans were finalized for a new restaurant called the Sea Wolf.

Shortly before Christmas in 1950, as the Sea Wolf lease was being negotiated, the commissioners adopted a resolution designating the waterfront blocks between Broadway and Webster Street "Jack London Square." In addition to paying homage to Oakland's most famous son, the name evoked the city's colorful past. History was on the minds of many Californians then, with centennial celebrations recently completed or underway for the Gold Rush, statehood, and dozens of counties and cities.

The formal dedication of Jack London Square took place on May 1, 1951, a date chosen to coincide with "the 99th anniversary of the birthplace of the City of Oakland." Though there was little to dedicate except a construction site, *Oakland Tribune* publisher Joseph R. Knowland unveiled a plaque commemorating "the establishment of Jack London Square by the Board of Port Commissioners of the City of Oakland . . . in honor of those citizens who in 1925 inaugurated the movement for creation of the Port of Oakland and who have since cooperated in its continued development." One of London's daughters attended; the writer, were he alive, would have been seventy-five.

Resolution on Jack London Square

Whereas, the Port Area between Broadway and Webster Street, lying south of First Street, has been associated with a great many of the major events in the life of Jack London as a youth and a writer of world renown; and

Whereas, it was the scene of his early adventures among the fishermen and oyster pirates of San Francisco Bay, and where he gained his first abiding interest in learning and the writer's profession from the old dictionary in the historic First and Last Chance Saloon of his friend and benefactor, the late John Heinold; and

Whereas, it was the general departure point for his many voyages to Alaska and the other ports of the Seven Seas, as well as the later cruises of his famous wind ship, the Snark; *and*

Whereas, it has become a mecca throughout the years for tourists with an abiding love of Jack London and his works; now, therefore, be it

RESOLVED that, in honor of the famous creator of The Sea-Wolf, Burning Daylight, The Call of the Wild *and* Martin Eden, *the Oakland Board of Port Commissioners hereby, for posterity, confers the designation "Jack London Square" upon the area of the City of Oakland between Broadway and Webster Street, First Street, and the Oakland Estuary.*

Resolution No. B1348
Oakland Board of Port Commissioners
Room 75, Grove Street Pier
December 4, 1950

But especially he loved to run in the dim twilight of the summer midnights, listening to the subdued and sleepy murmurs of the forest, reading signs and sounds as a man may read a book, and seeking for the mysterious something that called—called, waking or sleeping, at all times, for him to come.

— The Call of the Wild (1903)

Day by day he worked on, and day by day the postman delivered to him rejected manuscripts. He had no money for stamps, so the manuscripts accumulated in a heap under the table. Came a day when for forty hours he had not tasted food.

— Martin Eden (1909)

I stowed a roll of blankets and some cold food into a borrowed Whitehall boat and set sail. Out of the Oakland Estuary I drifted on the last of an early morning ebb, caught the first of the flood up the bay, and raced along with the spanking breeze.

— John Barleycorn (1913)

Jack London

In less than two decades Jack London produced over fifty volumes of novels, short stories, and essays. Enormously popular in his own day, he has retained a worldwide audience and is often cited as the most widely translated of American authors.

Born in San Francisco in 1876, London spent his boyhood in farming towns around the bay. The family settled in Oakland in 1886, leading a precarious existence without a fixed residence or regular income. Jack helped by delivering newspapers and sweeping saloon floors, later finding employment as a deckhand and factory laborer. His empathy for working men and women led him, at age twenty, to join the Socialist Labor Party, and as a Socialist he would run twice for the office of mayor of Oakland.

Largely self-taught, he discovered books at Oakland's public libraries. The winter of 1897–98, spent in the Yukon, served as the inspiration for his early fiction. His first book, a collection of Klondike tales, was published in 1900, when he was twenty-four. *The Call of the Wild* (1903), which made him famous, was followed by *The Sea-Wolf* (1904), *White Fang* (1906), *The Iron Heel* (1907), *Martin Eden* (1909), and other best-sellers. He died in 1916 at age forty, having spent his final years on his ranch in Sonoma County.

London virtually grew up on Oakland's waterfront. A favorite haunt was the old municipal wharf—now the heart of Jack London Square—where, at age fifteen, he briefly joined a gang of oyster pirates who raided the commercial beds in San Leandro Bay. The wharf also served as the starting point in 1907 for his two-year cruise to the South Pacific on the *Snark*.

The oldest building in Jack London Square is Heinold's First and Last Chance, a waterfront saloon opened in the 1880s by London's friend John Heinold. Still on its original site and little changed, the tavern was once adjoined by the Webster Street Bridge (thus offering imbibers their "first and last chance" for a drink in Oakland). London spent many hours at Heinold's, where he met colorful characters who figured in his stories. The building has been designated a National Literary Landmark.

Near Heinold's is a rebuilt log cabin, lived in by London during the Klondike gold rush. (His signature and the words "author, miner, Jan. 27, 1898" are scratched on one wall.) Acquired by the Port of Oakland, the cabin was brought south from the Yukon in 1969. Half of the original logs were used to create a replica cabin in Dawson City, Canada.

Opening for Business

In the year following the dedication, the Port rushed construction in anticipation of Oakland's centennial celebration of May 1–4, 1952. Jack London Square was to serve as one of the main venues, and it was completed just in time. Four new or refurbished restaurants—the Sea Food Grotto, Showboat, Sea Wolf, and Bow & Bell—lined the estuary waterfront, adjoined by a large parking lot and new streets, sidewalks, and streetlights. By prior agreement, all landscaping was carried out by the Oakland Park Department under the supervision of William Penn Mott, Jr.

The focal point of the development was the Sea Wolf, opened days before the centennial. Designed by Oakland architect Harry Bruno, the building conveyed "a windswept, driftwood impression . . . with its long sloping roof and many sharp angles," noted the magazine *Architect & Engineer*. A tower enhanced its prominence. The other new restaurant was the Showboat, a converted river steamer berthed next to the Sea Wolf; opened on New Year's Day in 1952, the boat burned and sank late in 1956. (The Paddle Wheel, formerly the ferry *Charles Van Damme*, opened at the same spot in 1958, followed by yet another Showboat in the 1960s.) The Bow & Bell and the newly remodeled Sea Food Grotto stood at either end of the row. Within a few years, two other restaurants, Simon's on the Square (later the Elegant Farmer) and London House, would open a block or two from the waterfront.

Jack London Square, 1952. The Bow & Bell, Sea Wolf, Showboat, and Oakland Sea Food Grotto line the waterfront from Broadway to Franklin Street. The parking lot lies across the Embarcadero (First Street) from the old Southern Pacific passenger depot. Fronting on Water and Webster Streets (right) are the Haslett Warehouse and the Inland Waterways Terminal.

Clyde
SUNDERLAND

A success from the beginning, Jack London Square was soon drawing a million annual visitors. Entertainment became part of doing business at the square. Flower festivals, water shows, harbor cruises, and outdoor theater (performed by the London Circle Players) were typical for the time. In 1955, the Port instituted the Jack London Square Art Festival in conjunction with the Oakland Chamber of Commerce, Oakland Art Museum, and California College of Arts and Crafts. Held every summer through 1970, the two-day event brought out as many as 50,000 persons to see paintings by hundreds of Bay Area artists. The most enduring tradition revolves around Christmas. Every holiday season since 1953 the Port has installed a giant evergreen (typically a Sierra white fir) at the foot of Broadway, and the tree-lighting ceremony is the occasion for carols and visits from Santa.

Jack London Square's new restaurants, the Sea Wolf and the Showboat (inserts), as they appeared in 1952.

Expansion

Planned as a small commercial enclave, Jack London Square soon grew to include a dozen restaurants adjoined by specialty shops, offices, a hotel, marinas, and a television studio and convention center. By the late 1960s, the district spread along four blocks of the waterfront, attracting several million visitors a year.

Two major projects in the 1950s extended the development beyond Broadway to Clay Street, two blocks to the west. In 1957, Oakland's first television station, KTVU–Channel 2, negotiated a lease for a building at the foot of Washington Street. The station began broadcasting from its new studios in July 1958. The second project, completed late in 1959, was a convention and banquet building at First and Washington Streets, next door to KTVU. Known as Goodman's Hall (or Jack London Hall), the facility was developed by the Port expressly for lease to the Goodman Catering Company, operators of the Bow & Bell; the building could accommodate gatherings of up to 1,000 persons. In conjunction with these projects, two block-sized parking lots went in between Broadway and Clay Street.

Jack London Square also expanded eastward, in tandem with the construction of the Webster Street Tube by the State of California. Opened in 1963, the new estuary tunnel to Alameda brought change to the Oakland waterfront. Between 1958 and 1960, as part of the right-of-way proceedings, the Port was required to demolish the Inland Waterways Terminal and the east third of the Haslett Warehouse (which the Port had acquired in 1956).

1952 tourist map by the Hubbard Advertising Agency. (Courtesy of Ernest T. Hubbard, Jr.)

The Port commissioners began studying possible uses for the vacated warehouse in 1957. It was decided that the Port's administrative offices would occupy the third floor; tenants would lease the remaining space. The contract for the remodeling was awarded late in 1960. With its veneer of aluminum panels and bands of horizontal windows, the new Port of Oakland Building (66 Jack London Square) bore little resemblance to the 1920s warehouse. Port employees made the five-block move from the Grove Street Pier in December 1961.

As the largest office and retail building in the area, 66 Jack London Square housed a variety of businesses. Two restaurants, the first of many in the building, opened in the early 1960s. The Mikado featured Japanese decor handcrafted in Japan and reassembled in Oakland. The rooftop Castaway, with a Polynesian theme, occupied a new penthouse served by a glass elevator. Other early tenants included an imports store, a chandlery, and radio station KNEW. The International Trade Center, opened in 1966 on the second floor, brought together firms and agencies involved in foreign trade: freight forwarders, customhouse brokers, banking services, and U.S. Customs, which moved over from the Grove Street Pier.

Before-and-after views of the Haslett Warehouse in 1961, during its remodeling as the Port of Oakland Building. The rounded forms in the top view are precast concrete sections for the new tube.

Looking over the promenade from the Port Building to the east basin of the marina, circa 1970. The two-story office building at 77 Jack London Square and the Metropolitan Yacht Club (with turret) adjoin The Mast restaurant.

Architect's rendering of the Boatel, with the KTVU studios and Goodman's Hall as a backdrop. In the 1980s, the Boatel was enlarged and renamed the Waterfront Plaza Hotel.

Shoreline Improvements

The Port Building, Goodman's Hall, and KTVU set the stage for the full development of Jack London Square in the 1960s. New projects focused on the shoreline. A 1959 consultant's report proposed a marina, yacht club, and waterfront hotel for the area. The Port would undertake dredging and riprapping; all other work was to be handled by lessees. In 1960, the shoreline lease was awarded to Mardeco, a development firm whose partners included marina operators and yacht brokers.

Work began on the marina in 1961; completed in 1964, the 200 berths occupied two basins extending west from Washington Street and east from Franklin Street. Several years later, Mardeco developed a cluster of buildings at the east end of the marina, including a yacht club, an office building, and a restaurant (The Mast, now Il Pescatore) off the end of Webster Street.

The other major shoreline project of the period was the Boatel, an eighty-three-room hotel with berths for yachts and a pool perched above the estuary. Owned and operated by the Clyde Gibb Company, the hotel opened in 1964 at the foot of Washington Street. (That same year, the privately developed, 110-room Jack London Inn opened on the site of the Southern Pacific passenger depot at the Embarcadero and Broadway.) Also at this time, the Sea Food Grotto was replaced with a new restaurant called the Grotto (now Kincaid's). Harry Bruno, Mardeco's design partner, also drew the plans for the Boatel and Grotto in addition to the earlier Sea Wolf, Goodman's Hall, and Port of Oakland Building, leaving his imprint on much of Jack London Square.

A wide promenade (created by closing Water Street in front of the Port of Oakland Building) led past the marina to Heinold's. The 1970 dedication of Jack London's Klondike cabin, on the inland side of the mall, served as a capstone to the early development of Jack London Square. With the exception of a large Cost Plus imports store at the west end of the square, and the Jack London Village complex to the east (both opened in 1975), no projects of consequence would be undertaken until the 1980s. Before looking at these recent developments, we need to examine the Port's other major ventures in commercial real estate.

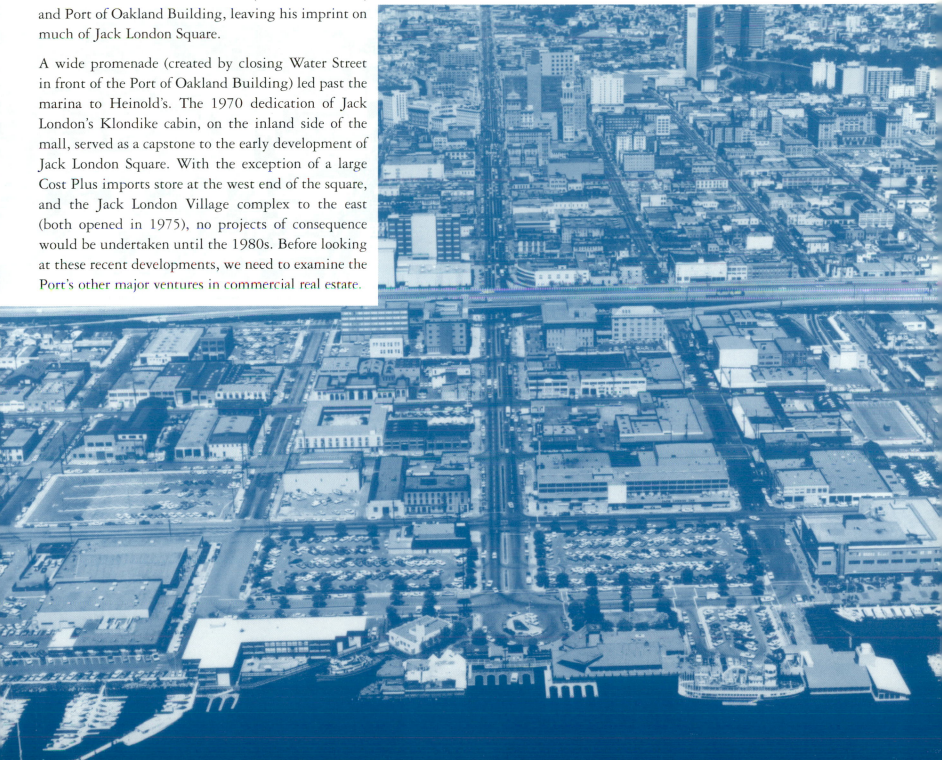

Jack London Square, 1966. KTVU, Goodman's Hall, and the Boatel are clustered at the foot of Washington Street (left). Broadway terminates at the Bow & Bell and Sea Wolf (center), adjoined by the new Showboat and Grotto (right). Jack London Inn and the Port of Oakland Building border the original parking lot.

Oakland Airport Business Park

Formerly known as the Port of Oakland Industrial Park, this 300-acre complex on San Leandro Bay is about the same age as Jack London Square. Site acquisition and reclamation began in the 1940s although construction did not get underway until the 1960s. Renamed the Oakland Airport Business Park in 1975, the development contains approximately 100 buildings ranging from small retail outlets and light-manufacturing plants to warehouses and office towers. Uniform setbacks, extensive landscaping, and attractive architecture provide a pleasant work environment for over 400 firms employing approximately 8,000 people.

Early Development

The Oakland Airport Business Park had its origins during World War II, when the Port of Oakland acquired approximately 950 acres of marsh and tideland on San Leandro Bay, north of Oakland Municipal Airport. Purchased in 1944 and 1945 from the E. B. & A. L. Stone Company and several other tax-delinquent owners, the site was slated for development as a twenty-eight-berth seaport and industrial complex, in accordance with the Port's 1944 Master Plan.

The Port's first conceptual plan for San Leandro Bay.

136

In the spring of 1948, a contract for dredging and filling 177 acres of marshland at the northeast corner of San Leandro Bay was awarded to the San Francisco Bridge Company (the same firm that had excavated a portion of the tidal canal). Completed early in 1949, the reclamation project was intended as the first phase in the overall development of the maritime-industrial complex. Bounded on the north by the unfinished East Shore Freeway, on the east by Hegenberger Road, on the south by the straightened channel of San Leandro Creek, and on the west by Damon Slough, this tract became the nucleus of the Business Park.

Of critical importance to the project—and to the Port at large—was the East Shore Freeway, the East Bay's first postwar highway. Later known as the Nimitz (Interstate 880), the six-lane corridor vastly improved access to the Outer and Inner Harbors, the airport, and San Leandro Bay. The Port helped plan the route through Oakland and provided land for the right-of-way. Construction began in 1946; by 1950 the highway had been opened south to the new overpass and ramps at Hegenberger Road.

Reclamation on San Leandro Bay, January 1949. The straightened channel of San Leandro Creek separates Arrowhead Marsh (left) from the diked area that is traversed by the Elmhurst Channel (center). The unfinished East Shore Freeway (right) cuts across the marshland to Hegenberger Road. (Courtesy of Pacific Aerial Surveys.)

137

The ambitious development program for San Leandro Bay languished for nearly a decade while the Port focused its attention on Jack London Square and airport expansion. In 1956—with reclamation underway for the airport and the freeway nearing completion to San Jose—the Board of Port Commissioners revived the project by requesting a feasibility study from the Stanford Research Institute (SRI), as recommended by Executive Director Dudley Frost.

SRI's initial study, submitted late in 1956, concluded that San Leandro Bay was "pre-eminently suited" for development as an industrial center, due to its location in a rapidly urbanizing area served by freeway and airport. The final report, completed a year later, contained suggestions for organizing, promoting, and developing the "Port of Oakland Industrial Park." These recommendations (including the proposed name) were formally adopted by the Port commissioners late in 1957. SRI also commented favorably on the long-term feasibility of a deep-water terminal on San Leandro Bay, but containerization soon rendered this component of the plan obsolete.

By Port policy, all buildings in the Industrial Park were to be financed by outside capital. The Port would provide land (for lease or sale) in parcels of one or more acres; private investors would be responsible for construction. Each lease or deed contained restrictions relating to use, setback, height, parking, and landscaping. While architectural plans required Port approval, most design decisions were left to the discretion of the developer. Driving through the area today, one is struck by the wide range of styles, from sleek modernism to woodsy suburbanism; yet the buildings are unified by their careful siting and landscaped setting.

Two "financially attractive" projects recommended by SRI—a "de luxe motor hotel" and a "modern produce center"—were given a high priority by the Port. In 1958, bids were invited for a motel near the Hegenberger overpass; the ground lease was awarded the following year. Completed in the fall of 1961, at a cost of $2.5 million, the 175-room Edgewater Inn represented the first major investment at the Industrial Park. Edgewater Drive took its name from the project.

By contrast, the "modern produce center" proved a costly failure. Known as the Pacific Coast Wholesale Food Terminal, this huge complex of food stalls, cold-storage plants and support facilities was to have been the centerpiece of the Industrial Park, covering more than 170 acres south of Edgewater Drive and San

Leandro Creek (including all of Arrowhead Marsh). In 1960, a developer secured the lease and prepared a master plan. The project died a sudden death late in 1961 when the Oakland Wholesale Fruit and Produce Merchants Association, in protest against the proposed high rents, refused to move from the existing Produce Market near Jack London Square.

In the three years following the opening of the Edgewater Inn, only a handful of leases were signed and fewer than five buildings were erected, despite a phased program of site improvements begun in 1959. Financed by Port revenue bonds, contracts were awarded for roads and utilities in thirty-acre increments west from Hegenberger Road. By 1964 the infrastructure was in place as far as the Elmhurst Channel. The major new roads—Edgewater Drive, at the center of the tract, and Oakport Street, bordering the freeway—ran west from Hegenberger. Smaller interior streets (named for past Port commissioners) included Leet Drive, Pendleton Way, Capwell Drive, and Roland Way.

A related development from this period was the Coliseum Complex. In 1963, the Board of Port Commissioners agreed to transfer 157 acres of Industrial Park property (mostly unreclaimed marshland west of the filled area) to the Oakland City Council, which conveyed the land to the East Bay Municipal Utility District (EBMUD). In exchange, EBMUD deeded to the city a 105-acre parcel north of the Nimitz Freeway which became the site of the Oakland–Alameda County Coliseum. Opened in 1966, the elegant stadium and arena attracted national attention as well as two championship teams with a style all their own—the Oakland Raiders and the Oakland A's.

In 1964, the Industrial Park was mostly vacant land. The partially completed Edgewater Drive (center) adjoins the angled form of the Edgewater Inn. Opened in 1961, the motel (insert) was demolished in 1997 to create a site for new development near the freeway.

139

Intensive Growth

The demise of the wholesale food terminal project, coupled with the generally slow pace of development, raised serious questions about the viability of the Industrial Park. The Port considered several remedies, including selling the property. In 1964, the Board of Port Commissioners petitioned the City Council for changes to the city charter that would allow greater flexibility in leasing and selling land. Specifically, it was requested that the term of Port leases be extended from fifty to sixty-six years in order to facilitate private financing; that the time-consuming process of competitive bids for leases be eliminated; and that the Port be permitted to sell land without the case-by-case concurrence of the city. The charter amendments were placed on the ballot and approved by the voters in the spring of 1965. Later that year, following months of negotiations with a Boston development firm, the commissioners decided not to sell the Industrial Park.

Looking south over the Industrial Park to Arrowhead Marsh and the airport, 1968. Across the Nimitz Freeway from the Coliseum Complex is the newly completed plant of the American Toy Company, later acquired by Grand Auto.

SUTHERLAND AERIAL PHOTOGRAPHS
Oakland, California

Empowered by the new charter provisions, the Port of Oakland launched an aggressive marketing campaign. Between 1965 and 1972, most remaining land within the Industrial Park was sold, and more than sixty buildings were erected. In 1966, the Port allocated $2.1 million in federal funds to extend site improvements to the filled area west of the Elmhurst Channel. Roadwork, utilities, grading, and remedial shoreline reclamation were completed several years later.

Occupying a twelve-acre site in the newly opened tract was the 300,000-square-foot warehouse of the American Toy Company, the largest building in the Industrial Park at the time of its completion in 1968. Another major project from this period was the Airport Office Center on Hegenberger Road. Developed by Stolte, an Oakland-based construction firm, the center comprised two speculative office buildings on a nine-acre site. The completion of the eight-story Wells Fargo

The Bank of America Building (1968) and Wells Fargo Bank Building (1972) comprise the Airport Office Center on Hegenberger Road.

The Industrial Park in November 1968. The first building at the Airport Office Center is finished. A domed theater adjoins the Edgewater Inn, and Edgewater Drive has been extended beyond the Elmhurst Channel to the American Toy Company's regional distribution center.

Building, late in 1972, coincided with the project's formal dedication by U.S. Transportation Secretary John A. Volpe.

In 1975, the Board of Port Commissioners voted to change the name of the Port of Oakland Industrial Park to the Oakland Airport Business Park. The new name reflected the development's increasingly nonindustrial character (functionally and visually) as well as its marketable proximity to Oakland International Airport. The Business Park was then home to over 200 firms and organizations, including corporate headquarters, branch offices, professional practices, fraternal and labor groups, regional distribution facilities, and retail establishments.

Infill construction continued strong through the 1980s, until relatively few vacant parcels were left. The development of office space for lease or sale has been the principal type of investment in recent years. The prime example is the $25 million Oakland Executive Center, developed in 1981–82 by the Equitec Financial Group. Overlooking I-880 from Oakport Street, the twelve-story office tower remains the tallest structure in the Business Park.

Buildings of the Business Park
(counterclockwise from top): (1) Safeway Stores data-processing center (1967), and Roll Rite (1965), manufacturers and distributors of industrial wheels and casters. (2) East Bay Center for Warehouse Union, Local 6, ILWU, Hegenberger Road at Pardee Drive (1965); designed by Oakland architect Herbert T. Johnson, the building features an unusual roof-support system of steel arches and cables, and is richly adorned with mosaic panels. (3) Garden-court complex of speculative office buildings developed by Ryan, Marocco & Company (1971). (4) Pacific Intermountain Express (P.I.E.) Credit Union (1967). (5) Equitec's Oakland Executive Center (1982).

The Oakland Airport Business Park, 1993. (Courtesy of Pacific Aerial Surveys.)

143

The Oakland Airport Hilton soon after its completion in 1970, looking west over the vacant Distribution Center tract. Occupying a twenty-acre site at Hegenberger Road and Doolittle Drive, the 365-room facility was Oakland's first major hotel in decades.

Port of Oakland Distribution Center

That portion of the Business Park lying south of San Leandro Creek, inland from Hegenberger Road and Doolittle Drive, is known as the Port of Oakland Distribution Center. Covering approximately 125 acres, the area was originally intended as a 200-acre support facility for air-cargo operations at the airport, with sites reserved for firms dealing in airborne freight. To date, the only such firm to have made a major investment is United Parcel Service.

The Port announced plans for the Distribution Center in 1968; by 1971, most of Arrowhead Marsh had been filled for the project. Pardee Drive and Swan Way (named for former commissioners) were cut through the tract. In 1975, United Parcel Service undertook the first development, a regional truck terminal which enabled UPS to commence air-cargo operations at Oakland. Later developments in the area include a branch post office, a fire station, several speculative office buildings, and a FedEx customer service center operated in conjunction with the company's sort facility at the airport.

The Distribution Center in 1986. UPS's parcel-handling facility (center) borders the San Leandro Creek Channel. The year this picture was taken, environmental groups sued the Port over the filling of wetlands; the 1994 settlement resulted in the wetlands restoration of most of the vacant property west of UPS.

144

In this 1964 view, the marshland site of the Port of Oakland Distribution Center extends south from the San Leandro Creek Channel. The inserts show the marsh diked but still intact in 1968 (top), and filled in 1972 (bottom).

145

Embarcadero Cove

By the late 1970s, the Business Park and Jack London Square were virtually complete, pending infill construction and redevelopment. It was during these years that the Port undertook a new project called Embarcadero Cove—the collective name for various commercial properties on the shore of Brooklyn Basin.

Antecedents

Comprising about a mile of estuary shoreline, the crescent-shaped cove is the site of the East Bay's earliest maritime activity. It was here, during the Spanish-Mexican period, that the Embarcadero de San Antonio was established at the cove's midpoint. Soon after the Gold Rush, two pioneer settlements in the area merged to form the town of Brooklyn, later annexed to Oakland. By World War I, boat yards, lumber yards, and manufacturing plants lined the shore opposite the newly created Government Island (now Coast Guard Island). The cove's protected waters also served as a graveyard for abandoned square-riggers.

Brooklyn Basin in the 1930s, looking west up the estuary. The triangular moorage in the foreground is the Oakland Yacht Harbor; Ninth Avenue Terminal is at the far end of the basin. Note the square-riggers berthed off Government Island.

Looking north over Brooklyn Basin and Coast Guard Island, 1993. The Port's Embarcadero Cove marinas line the shore; the marinas in the foreground are in Alameda. (Courtesy of Pacific Aerial Surveys.)

The Port of Oakland maintained three Inner Harbor facilities on Brooklyn Basin: two early wharves to the east, at Livingston and Dennison Streets, and the Ninth Avenue Terminal at the basin's west end. The Port's 1944 Master Plan called for a new terminal in the area (which was never built) as well as a new roadway—the Embarcadero—to improve access between the harbor and the proposed East Shore Freeway (I-880). Constructed in the early 1950s, the Embarcadero hugs the Oakland shoreline at Brooklyn Basin and crosses the Lake Merritt Channel to merge with First Street (renamed the Embarcadero).

Recreational Development

The Port's very first recreational project was located in Brooklyn Basin. Opened in 1930, the Oakland Yacht Harbor—the estuary's first public marina—adjoined the moorage of the Oakland Yacht Club at the foot of Nineteenth Avenue, and was operated under lease by the club. The completion of the Embarcadero attracted other commercial marinas. Don Durant's Embarcadero Cove project of 1969–70 set the tone for the area's later development. The complex of restaurants, shops, offices, and 150-berth marina was built on a five-acre, Port-leased site next to the Oakland Yacht Harbor. The complex is notable as an early East Bay example of adaptive reuse (adapting old buildings to new uses). Structures moved to the site include a train station and Victorian houses (used for offices) and a turn-of-the-century lighthouse (now a restaurant) that once stood at the mouth of the estuary.

The original Embarcadero Cove development features a 1903 lighthouse barged to the site in 1970 (above) and several Victorian houses converted to offices (below).

In the 1970s, the Port of Oakland undertook a redevelopment of the Brooklyn Basin waterfront, borrowing the name Embarcadero Cove for the overall project. Financed by loans from the State Department of Navigation and Ocean Development, and completed in phases between 1977 and 1990, the improvements included marinas, parking lots, sidewalks, streetlights, and shoreline paths. The Oakland Yacht Harbor was razed, requiring the Oakland Yacht Club to move across the estuary to new facilities in Alameda. The three new marinas—North Basin, Central Basin, and Union Point Basin—comprise more than 450 berths. Associated ground-lease projects include motels, office buildings, and restaurants. Like Jack London Square, the transformation of Brooklyn Basin from working waterfront to recreational waterway has been dramatic.

Rendering of the new KTVU studio complex. Spanke, Lynd and Sprague, architects.

Recent Developments and Future Plans

The Port of Oakland has major projects planned or underway at Embarcadero Cove, the Oakland Airport Business Park, and Jack London Square. New and expanded hotel facilities and shoreline amenities are planned for Embarcadero Cove. At the Business Park, about seventy-five acres of Port-owned land are currently for sale; preferred uses include hotels, offices, and service-related businesses. The Hegenberger Corridor Development Plan, devised jointly with the city of Oakland, seeks to transform Hegenberger Road and nearby Ninety-eighth Avenue into stylish gateways serving the airport.

Jack London Square has been the focus of most recent development. In the 1960s, the Port began studying the area east of the square for expansion. Most of the half-mile of waterfront between Harrison Street and the Lake Merritt Channel was owned by the Santa Fe Railroad. In 1964, Santa Fe announced plans for a forty-five-acre complex of high-rise apartments and marinas; a third of the site was to be leased from the Port, which considered the project compatible with Jack London Square. Santa Fe ultimately built a scaled-down version, the 300-unit Portobello, which opened in 1973 on a thirty-acre site near the Lake Merritt Channel.

In 1972, Specialty Restaurants Corporation, of Long Beach, California, signed a lease with the Port for two acres at the foot of Alice Street. Jack London Village, a rustic compound of shops and restaurants, opened on the site in 1975. In 1979, Santa Fe sold the Port a sixteen-acre parcel bordered by Portobello and Jack London Village—the last vacant tract between Jack

Jack London Village, soon after its opening in 1975. The rustic complex of shops and restaurants was designed by Frank Laulainen & Associates, in collaboration with Frank and Caree Rose.

London Square and the Lake Merrit Channel. The east third of this property became KTVU's new studio complex, opened in 1981. A 1980 proposal for the remaining ten acres envisioned a $114 million hotel-office complex to serve as the new focal point of Jack London Square. The property was later sold to a private developer, and in 1999 construction started on a 288-unit apartment complex.

During the 1980s, the Port shifted the focus of its Jack London Square planning from off-site expansion to on-site reconstruction. The Phase I Master Plan, adopted in 1984 by the Board of Port Commissioners, called for major new office and retail space and parking facilities in an eight-block area between Franklin and Clay Streets. The Port would contribute $30 million to develop public outdoor areas and two garages. Private developers would finance, construct, and manage the buildings. Difficulties in financing the $100 million undertaking finally compelled the Port to acquire an effective 100 percent interest in Oakland Portside Associates, the project developer.

The new plaza, with the gabled Pavilion Building (now Barnes & Noble) as a backdrop.

Begun in 1986, the redevelopment of Jack London Square was largely completed by 1990. The project's centerpiece is a landscaped plaza (with underground garage), opened in 1987 and 1988 on the site of the original parking lot. Parking is also provided by a seven-level structure on Washington Street. Five new buildings, including the new Port of Oakland Building, contain more than 300,000 square feet of office and retail space. The only older structures still standing in the project area are the Sea Wolf (Scott's), the Grotto (Kincaid's), and the Boatel, reconstructed as the 144-room Waterfront Plaza Hotel.

Jack London Square has also been enhanced with ferry and train service. Transbay ferry service was revived in 1989, after the Loma Prieta earthquake damaged the lower deck of the Bay Bridge. The Blue & Gold Fleet runs its ferries between San Francisco and Oakland via Alameda, and also provides summer service to Angel

Formally dedicated on March 22, 1990, the Port of Oakland Building at 530 Water Street is the principal landmark in the redeveloped Jack London Square. The building has a metal-clad exterior, a copper roof, and interior public spaces incorporating works by local artists. Designed by IDG Architects, the seven-story structure overlooks the site of the old Port headquarters at the Grove Street Pier (now Charles P. Howard Terminal).

Island. A new ferry terminal opened at the west end of the square in 1992. The earthquake also damaged Oakland's main passenger depot at Sixteenth and Wood Streets, disrupting Amtrak service. A new station, built by the Port with state funding, opened in 1995 just east of the square. Designed by VBN Architects, the vaulted glass-and-steel structure is named in honor of civil rights leader Cottrell L. Dellums (1900–1989), an Oakland resident who cofounded the Brotherhood of Sleeping Car Porters, the nation's first African-American labor union.

Other recent projects include the nine-screen Jack London Cinema (1995) and a totally reconstructed marina (completed in 2000). The marina, which includes a new harbormaster's building, provides ample public access to the waterfront via promenades, walkways, and piers. (The project required the removal of shoreline structures east of Webster Street, notably the Metropolitan Yacht Club and 77 Jack London Square.) The Phase II Master Plan calls for a major new complex in this area, combining hotel, retail, office, and entertainment uses. The Estuary Policy Plan also proposes an expansion of Jack London Square up Broadway to I-880, where the space under the elevated freeway would be redesigned as a gateway linking the city's downtown with its waterfront.

Although little remains of the original waterfront district except Heinold's First and Last Chance, the historic shoreline environment is evoked by plaques, sculpture, and a self-guided tour, along which visitors are led by bronze wolf-tracks and markers bearing the names of their sponsors. The U.S.S. *Potomac*, the 165-foot yacht used by President Franklin D. Roosevelt as his floating White House, is berthed at the west end of the square. Acquired by the Port in 1980, and restored at a cost of $5 million, the vessel has been designated a National Historic Landmark. It is managed by the Association for the Preservation of the Presidential Yacht Potomac, and is open for dockside tours, narrated cruises, and educational events. Over 50,000 people have visited the ship since its public opening in 1995.

Jack London Square has emerged as a strong and attractive entertainment and business center in the greater Bay Area. Major tenants such as the Jack London Cinema (currently drawing over a million annual customers), Barnes & Noble, and Yoshi's jazz club add to the district's allure. Dozens of events are staged each year, from boat shows to outdoor concerts, and the annual Italian Festa, Fourth of July fireworks, and holiday tree-lighting have become community traditions. This renewed vitality should assure Jack London Square's continued role as the most popular gathering place on Oakland's waterfront.

The U.S.S. Potomac *off Jack London Square, 1995.*

C. L. Dellums Amtrak Station, Alice and Second Streets, Jack London Square. This 1995 view, taken soon after the station opened, looks south to the pedestrian bridge over the tracks.

Community Design Fair, Port View Park, August 30, 1998. Hundreds of Oakland residents attended this Port-sponsored event to learn about the Middle Harbor Shoreline Park and Enhancement Area, and to provide input for the design process. Historical photographs from the Port of Oakland Archives were displayed on the upper floor of the park building, formerly a railroad interlocking tower at the Southern Pacific's Oakland Mole.

uring its first four decades, the Port of Oakland perceived its mission almost exclusively in terms of "commerce and navigation," its original mandate under state and city law. In this traditional approach, the waterfront was treated as an economic resource—a place set apart for shipping, industry, and commercial development.

Since the 1960s, broad-based concerns for social issues and environmental quality have changed the way the Port conducts its affairs. Concepts such as equal opportunity, economic parity, citizen participation, and public access have been translated into policy and practice, and the environmental movement has given rise to new methods of resource management and stewardship. Together, these forces have transformed the Port into an institution that is more accessible and more responsive than it has been at any time in its history.

The Port and the Community

The Port of Oakland is a complex institution with a complex mission. A major provider of transportation services, it is also a land developer. A department of the city government with a governing board appointed by the mayor and City Council, it is also an independent arm of that government with special powers under the city charter—a public agency operating as a self-supporting business.

With its jurisdiction over nineteen miles of Oakland waterfront, the Port controls all city-owned property and helps regulate all private property within a charter-defined district known as the Port Area. The Port exercises ownership rights over more than 5,000 acres of land and 10,000 acres of water, 90 percent of which has been granted "in trust" to the city of Oakland by the State of California. The Port acts on behalf of the city to manage these state lands (tidelands and former tidelands) which by law can only be used for "commerce, navigation, and fisheries." Legal interpretations over the years have clarified what uses are allowed, and these now include aviation, commercial real estate, and recreation.

Economic activities associated with the Port of Oakland comprise the city's largest source of employment. Directly and indirectly, the Port generates over 35,000 jobs in the Bay Area with a combined payroll of about $1.6 billion. Current expansion programs will create thousands of new positions in Port-related construction and industries. By Port policy, Oakland residents and businesses are actively recruited.

Henry J. Rodriguez

Thomas L. Berkley

Herbert Eng

Patricia Pineda

Christine Scotlan

One example is provided by the Vision 2000 Maritime Development Program. Under a master labor agreement, at least half of the construction jobs created by the expansion of marine and rail facilities will be reserved for local residents. Another example is the Hire Area Residents Program (HARP), which provides cash incentives to firms employing persons from economically disadvantaged sections of the Oakland vicinity. The city government has also received Port monies, including over $80 million in surplus revenues transferred to the city treasury to cover the remaining principal and interest on voter-approved bonds issued for Port purposes.

In 1969, the Port of Oakland became one of the first major ports to adopt an equal-opportunity policy "to protect and safeguard the right and opportunity of all persons to seek, obtain and hold employment without discrimination on account of race, color, religious creed, national origin, age, sex, handicap or veterans' status." This policy has since been modified to include marital status and sexual orientation. An affirmative-action policy adopted in 1973 seeks "to attract and maintain a ratio of minorities among Port of Oakland workers . . . generally equivalent to the ethnic composition of Oakland." Minority participation in the Port's work force increased from 24 percent in 1969 to 41 percent in 1973; the goal of equivalence was achieved in the early 1990s, at 64 percent. The policy is applied equally to hiring, contracts, purchases, and tenant selection.

Under a 1968 charter amendment, the Oakland Board of Port Commissioners was expanded from five to seven members, allowing more diverse representation from the community. (At the same time, terms were reduced from six to four years.) The first African American to sit on the Board, attorney and publisher Thomas L. Berkley, was appointed in 1969, followed by the first Latino member, Henry J. Rodriguez, in 1977, and the first Asian member, Herbert Eng, in 1979. Attorney Patricia Pineda, appointed in 1981 as the first female commissioner, went on to serve as the Board's first female president. She was joined in 1985 by Christine Scotlan, the first African American woman to sit on the Board of Port Commissioners.

Following the 1989 resignation of Walter Abernathy, American President Lines executive Nolan Gimpel was hired as the Port's executive director. Gimpel oversaw a restructured administration which placed a greater emphasis on commercial real estate. He was succeeded in 1991 by Charles Roberts, the Port's chief engineer and a veteran of the Army Corps of Engineers, who emphasized the Port's core business activities. Charles W. Foster succeeded Roberts in 1995. A retired Navy Reserve captain with a degree in public administration, Foster joined the Port in 1986 as director of aviation. He has promoted coalition-building with community and labor groups while striving to keep the Port competitive.

Charles W. Foster

Charles R. Roberts

Oakland Board of Port Commissioners, 1999. Standing, left to right: Peter Uribe, past commissioners James B. Lockhart and Celso D. Ortiz, President John Loh, Robert L. Harris, and David Kramer. Seated: Becky L. Taylor and Kathy Neal. Insert: Frank Kiang.

155

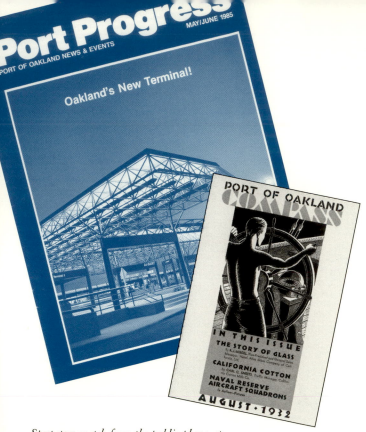

Spectators watch from the public plaza at Oakland Municipal Airport as Amelia Earhart's Lockheed Electra is readied for departure, March 1937. The Exhibit Building (rear) housed Weldon Cooke's biplane, the Diamond.

Public Outreach and Citizen Involvement

As a public agency, the Port of Oakland is in continual dialogue with the community. The twice-monthly public meetings of the Board of Port Commissioners provide a regular forum for discussion, as do the quarterly sessions of the Port–City Liaison Committee, when the Board sits in joint session with the Oakland City Council. For most of its history, the Port has also had an active public-relations department which interacts with the community through publications and special events.

The *Port of Oakland Compass*, published on a more-or-less monthly basis from 1932 to 1942, informed the public about Port activities. After World War II, the Port issued progress reports and newsletters, which gradually evolved into a magazine called *Port Progress* (renamed *Compass* in 1996). Brochures, directories, and other promotional items are distributed to the public on a regular basis, and the Port maintains a Web site on the Internet.

Over the years, special events have brought the public into contact with the Port's maritime and aviation activities. Oakland Municipal Airport, which hosted air shows on a frequent basis, also included passenger travel as part of its day-to-day operations. For this reason, the airport was quite accessible to visitors, even including a spectator's plaza on the flight line. By contrast, the working waterfront, characterized by cargo handling and industrial activity, posed a danger to public safety. The Port's marine terminals were not designed to accommodate daily visitors who wished to observe steamships and stevedores at close range.

Port-sponsored waterfront events began in the 1930s, when Navy vessels were customarily opened to the public on Navy Day and Armistice Day (now known as Veterans Day). The Port's oldest waterfront tradition is Port Day, staged in conjunction with National Maritime Day. First held between 1935 and 1940, and briefly revived after the war, Port Day was reinstituted as an annual event in the 1970s. The prewar gatherings included bus tours of the waterfront, tours of steamships, and a banquet in one of the Outer Harbor transit sheds. Port Day in its modern guise (1999's event was called Port Fest) offers harbor tours, boat races, entertainment, and displays pertaining to Port operations, drawing tens of thousands of vistors to Jack London Square.

Port of Oakland Day, circa 1940. Prior to World War II, the event included a civic banquet in one of the Outer Harbor transit sheds.

Promoting trade in the 1930s.

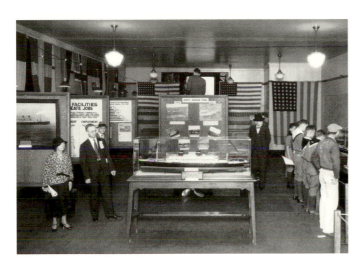

Port of Oakland display, 1930s.

Port Fest, Jack London Square, 1999.

The Navy cruiser U.S.S. Tuscaloosa at the Grove Street Pier, Navy Day, 1935.

Shoreline Access and Parkland

Public access to the waterfront is a central motif of recent Port history. Since the 1960s, an expanding network of paths and parkland has opened up miles of the city's shoreline for public use. Developed for the most part on former industrial sites, these open spaces tend to be small and urban in feeling, at times offering dramatic views of the Port's maritime operations. The major exception is San Leandro Bay, where a large park has been established to protect the last remnant of Oakland's natural shoreline.

The Port's traditional approach to shoreline access was commercial in nature. This is exemplifed by Jack London Square and Embarcadero Cove, where public amenities are interwoven with commercial uses. Marinas were among the earliest such uses. The Port opened the estuary's first public marina in 1930, and has since developed five marinas with about 650 berths. Today, the Oakland and Alameda shores of the estuary are home to a half-dozen yacht clubs and fifteen marinas totaling 3,500 berths—the largest concentration on San Francisco Bay.

In the 1960s, the Port's approach to public access began to move away from purely commercial ventures. The Port of Oakland Preliminary Master Development Plan (also known as the Oakland Shoreline Plan) signaled the shift in priorities. Completed by consultants Wilsey & Ham in 1968, this comprehensive overview—the Port's first since World War II—was commissioned "with a view toward maximizing recreational uses of Port property." Among its proposals, the plan envisaged promenades at the mouth of the estuary and wildlife refuges on San Leandro Bay.

The Port of Oakland undertook its first parkland developments at about the time of the Shoreline Plan. The earliest projects—Galbraith Golf Course, Port View Park, and Estuary Park—were conceived in largely commercial terms. The Lew F. Galbraith Memorial Golf Course, opened in 1966 on a 169-acre landfill site adjoining the airport, was built in collaboration with the city of Oakland as a revenue-producing project. The Port provided the land and funding; the city developed and operated the facility.

Whaleboats pass by Coast Guard Island in the Head of the Estuary Race, an annual rowing regatta on Port Day.

Galbraith Golf Course.

Port View Park was created in conjunction with the Seventh Street terminal complex, and it was the Port's first noncommercial public-access project. Not that it began that way: the original concept, in 1968, called for a revolving restaurant on the 2.5-acre site (an idea that was dropped due to cost). As built, the facility included a fishing pier and observation tower. Opened during the 1971 dedication of the Public Container Terminal, the park was closed in 1989 following the Loma Prieta earthquake (which damaged the Seventh Street peninsula). The park reopened in 1995 on a reconfigured 4.5-acre site to the east. It includes picnic tables, play equipment, sculptures, and a shoreline path leading to the original fishing pier. Two facilities have been moved to the park. A 1914 interlocking tower, which once routed trains at the Southern Pacific Mole, has been refurbished to house a snack bar, restrooms, and an upper-level observation room with historical displays. The International Maritime Center, currently in temporary quarters at Port View Park, provides religious services and hospitality for seafarers.

The interlocking tower being moved to Port View Park.

The San Francisco skyline forms a backdrop for the observation tower in old Port View Park.

159

Port View Park, 1999.

Estuary Park as it appeared soon after its opening in 1972, viewed from the Lake Merritt Channel.

Linked by a shoreline path to Jack London Square, Estuary Park opened in 1972 on a 7.5-acre site at the estuary's juncture with the Lake Merritt Channel. This park was another collaborative effort of the Port and the city of Oakland, whose Central District Plan called for a parkway in the area. Formerly a lumberyard, the site was donated by the Port, with major funding provided by state and federal grants. As designed by landscape architect Lawrence Halprin in 1968, the park was to have been a highly commercialized, sixteen-acre facility containing a parking structure, a fish market, a marina, and a restaurant perched atop a ten-story tower. The plan was scaled back in 1970 to the current configuration of playing field, picnic area, promenade, boat ramp, dock and fishing pier. A boating facility known as the Jack London Aquatic Center opened in the park in 2000.

During the 1970s, the Port developed a handful of smaller facilities unrelated to commercial uses. Radio Beach (formerly Northport Beach) is a short strip of bay shore adjoining the approach to the Bay Bridge. Alice Street Minipark is a quarter-acre landscaped area next to Jack London Village. Fruitvale Minipark offers views of the tidal canal from a platform by the Miller-Sweeney Bridge. Middle Harbor Park, with a picnic area and fishing pier, covers about an acre at the west edge of the American President Lines Terminal (formerly Middle Harbor Terminal). This park is to be closed and its site redeveloped for new marine terminals as part of the Vision 2000 program; the much larger Middle Harbor Shoreline Park will be built nearby.

San Leandro Bay, containing the last remnant of Oakland's natural shoreline, is unique among the Port's landholdings. Originally, this inlet of San Francisco Bay was bordered by over 2,000 acres of marshland, which remained largely intact through the 1920s. Due to intensive development in the area, only about seventy acres of pristine marsh survive today, now protected within the boundaries of the Martin Luther King, Jr., Regional Shoreline. The 1,220-acre park is managed by the East Bay Regional Park District; about half of the land and water acreage is leased from the Port of Oakland for a dollar a year.

The park was created in the aftermath of public outcry over the filling of marshland for the Distribution Center. In 1971, the year the fill was completed, the Port formed the Citizens' Advisory Group on San Leandro Bay Planning. The group's 1972 report, "Guidelines for San Leandro Bay," called for preservation of the area's remaining open space. In 1976, the Port agreed to lease 565 acres to the East Bay Regional Park District as partial mitigation for its proposed filling of wetlands at the airport. The city of Oakland's Bay Park Refuge (a five-acre facility at the end of Edgewater Drive) was incorporated into the new park. San Leandro Bay Regional Shoreline opened in phases, beginning in 1977 with a boat-launching facility and restaurant on Doolittle Drive. The Arrowhead Marsh wildlife refuge opened in the early 1980s; the bay's north shore, east of Damon Slough, was made fully accessible by the early 1990s. In 1992, the park was renamed in honor of the slain civil rights leader, who is also memorialized by a grove of trees.

The future of a major portion of Oakland's waterfront is addressed in the Estuary Policy Plan, a joint project of the city of Oakland and the Port, with Roma Design Group as principal consultant. Adopted in 1999 by the City Council and the Board of Port Commissioners, the study contains policies and implementation measures for a 5.5-mile stretch of shoreline extending from the vicinity of Jack London Square to San Leandro Bay. The plan calls for an unbroken band of parks, paths, and other public amenities which would form part of Oakland's contribution to the San Francisco Bay Trail—the half-completed, 400-mile corridor of bayshore open space being created under the auspices of the Association of Bay Area Governments.

The Estuary Policy Plan is evidence of the Port's growing commitment to community participation. The plan itself is an outgrowth of a 1993 study by the League of Women Voters ("The Waterfront: It Touches the World; How Does It Touch Oakland?"), and its preparation involved input from every major citizen group and public agency. The Waterfront Coalition—another outgrowth of the 1993 study, composed of more than thirty businesses and organizations—meets with the Port on a regular basis to promote the shoreline as a community asset.

Environmental sculpture, Martin Luther King, Jr., Regional Shoreline. Arrowhead Marsh (below) is the largest of several marshland areas within the park. (Courtesy of the East Bay Regional Park District.)

Marshland reclamation, San Leandro Bay, 1949. Arrowhead Marsh is partially visible in the foreground.

Stewardship

For much of its history, the Port of Oakland undertook projects with little or no review from regulatory agencies. Construction could proceed with remarkable speed. It took five years (1926–31) to create an entire maritime infrastructure, a little over two years (1927–29) to build a modern airport. Such efficiency, impressive as it is, exacted a price in terms of the environment. The airport, for example, was built at the expense of hundreds of acres of Bay Farm Island marsh, and its later expansion required the filling of 1,400 acres of San Francisco Bay. Tidelands and wetlands in those years were viewed no differently from upland sites—as resources to be used in the promotion of commerce and navigation.

Environmental legislation has transformed the way the Port manages its resources. The National Historic Preservation Act (1966), National Environmental Policy Act (1969), California Environmental Quality Act (1970), Clean Water Act (1972), and other statutes seek to protect and sustain a wide range of natural and cultural resources, from wetlands and wildlife habitats to historic structures and archeological sites. Under the provisions of the California Environmental Quality Act (CEQA) and the National Environmental Policy Act (NEPA), the Port is required to assess the effects of proposed projects on the environment. Reports are prepared by analyzing the effects and suggesting mitigation measures to avoid or reduce adverse impacts. For larger projects with demonstrated effects, an Environmental Impact Report (EIR) under CEQA or an Environmental Impact Statement (EIS) under NEPA is usually prepared (sometimes combined into a single EIR/EIS document). As a California public agency, the Port must comply with CEQA before any project is undertaken; compliance with NEPA is triggered by federal involvement. Impacts are evaluated from a variety of perspectives, including air and water quality, endangered species, habitats, noise, traffic,

Great Blue Heron

hazardous materials, and cultural resources. The reports are made available to the public and other agencies for comment and review.

The chief federal regulatory agency for most Port projects is the Army Corps of Engineers, which has jurisdiction over navigable waterways and wetlands. Other regulatory agencies include the Federal Aviation Administration, Environmental Protection Agency, U.S. Fish and Wildlife Service, State Department of Fish and Game, Caltrans, Regional Water Quality Control Board, and San Francisco Bay Conservation and Development Commission (BCDC). Established in 1965, BCDC regulates projects situated on the open bay and in a shoreline band extending 100 feet inland from the mean high-tide line.

Dredging is one of the costliest and most complex issues facing the Port, as Oakland lacks a naturally deep harbor. By the 1980s, environmental concerns and legal challenges meant that traditional methods of disposing of dredged materials were no longer feasible. Oakland's stalled forty-two-foot channel-deepening project was one of the factors prompting the Army Corps of Engineers and other agencies to establish a regional task force to study the problem. The resulting Long Term Management Strategy (LTMS) recommended that disposal activities be carried out in an environmentally sound manner, and that dredged materials be reused as a beneficial resource rather than being discarded as waste.

Two of the Port's disposal sites for the forty-two-foot deepening project exemplify these LTMS goals. At Galbraith Golf Course, where settling had marred the surface, the site was capped with dredged sediments which will be returfed for the course's reopening. In Sonoma County, near the mouth of the Petaluma River, dredged materials were used to create over 300 acres of tidal wetlands. Known as the Sonoma Baylands, the project received national praise at the time of its completion in 1997. The proposed fifty-foot channel-deepening project will reuse almost all of the dredged materials to restore wetlands or create shallow-water habitats at three locations around the bay: Oakland's Middle Harbor, Hamilton Field in Marin County, and Montezuma Slough in Solano County.

Projects like the Sonoma Baylands have given the Port of Oakland a national reputation for creativity in environmental compliance and stewardship. Other examples can be cited. The Martin Luther King, Jr., Regional Shoreline Wetlands Project resulted from litigation. Most of Arrowhead Marsh had been diked from

Filling in the bay for the Seventh Street terminal complex, 1967. This was one of the last large bayfill projects allowed under state legislation creating the San Francisco Bay Conservation and Development Commission.

Pickleweed

Middle Harbor Basin in the early 1930s, before the tideland shallows were filled and deepened for the Navy.

Middle Harbor Basin, April 1942. The basin has been partially filled and dredged for the Oakland Naval Supply Depot, later known as the Fleet & Industrial Supply Center, Oakland (FISCO). (Courtesy of the U.S. Navy.)

tidal action in the 1960s and filled in the early 1970s for the development of the Distribution Center. The largely vacant tract was in the process of reverting to wetland when the Port resumed filling in 1986, at the same time that wetland filling began at the airport. The Golden Gate Audubon Society and other environmental groups filed suit over inadequate environmental review by the Army Corps of Engineers (which issued the permits for the filling), halting both projects. The 1994 settlement required the Port to restore a portion of the Distribution Center site to wetland. Completed in 1998, the restoration involved the breaching of the exterior dike and the removal of fill material to allow tidal water to enter the area. The property has been turned over to the East Bay Regional Park District for long-term management as part of the Martin Luther King, Jr., Regional Shoreline.

The Berths 55–58 Project will create four new container berths on a portion of the site of the Fleet & Industrial Supply Center, Oakland. The Final EIR for the project includes dozens of environmental commitments valued at $55 million, nearly one-tenth of the total budget of the Vision 2000 Maritime Development Program. The innovative Vision 2000 Air Quality Mitigation Program will reduce pollutant emissions from increased shipping, cargo handling, rail movements, and truck traffic by replacing engines and installing emission-control devices. The proposed Middle Harbor Shoreline Park and Middle Harbor Enhancement Area will both reuse dredged materials to restore the old Middle Harbor basin (partially deepened for the Navy) to a semblance of the original tideland. The result will be a shallow-water wildlife habitat the size of Lake Merritt—about 190 acres—encircled by an approximately thirty-acre shoreline park. The design of the park resulted in large part from the input of local citizens and interest groups.

Adverse impacts to cultural resources (which include historic structures and archeological sites) range from alteration to destruction. For resources considered significant—that is, eligible for listing on the National Register of Historic Places—impacts require mitigation. In the case of demolition, this often takes the form of photographic and written documentation. The estuary's north training wall, constructed in the late nineteenth century as part of Oakland's federal harbor improvements, is a case in point. Deemed eligible for the National Register, the structure was documented prior to demolition for the Berths 55–58 Project, and a portion of the wall will be relocated and rebuilt in Middle Harbor Shoreline Park. Another example is provided by the 1995 demolition of a National Register-eligible transit shed at the Grove Street Pier. Mitigation measures included the documentation of the structure, the establishment of a Port archives, and the production of an illustrated history—the book you are now reading.

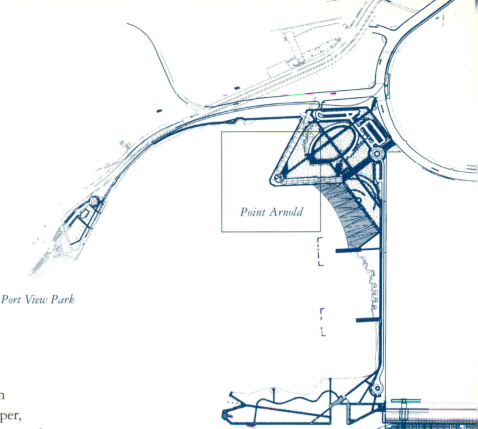

Port View Park

❦

The Port of Oakland embarks on the new century imbued with an awareness of its diverse roles as transportation provider, land developer, resource manager, and community participant. The core concerns of "commerce and navigation" continue to drive the Port's efforts to remain competitive in a global and regional market. Indeed, the current seaport and airport expansion programs constitute the greatest outlay of capital in Port history (about $1.6 billion), and are comparable in scale to the initial construction campaign of the 1920s. The Port's investment in commercial real estate is also unprecedented.

A public agency and a trustee of public lands, the Port has adopted increasingly sophisticated methods to manage its resources and fulfill its public-trust obligations. The transactions of the Board of Port Commissioners have become more open and responsive to civic concerns. The Port of Oakland and the city of Oakland are forging a closer, more collaborative relationship. As the inheritor of Oakland's waterfront—a role first played by Horace Carpentier, later by the Southern Pacific Railroad, and finally by the city itself—the Port has learned to balance commerce with community, development with stewardship. At this pivotal point in its history, the past and the future converge to shape its present course.

Configuration of the Middle Harbor Shoreline Park and Middle Harbor Enhancement Area, occupying a portion of the FISCO site. Park design by David L. Gates & Associates and Thruston Design Group.

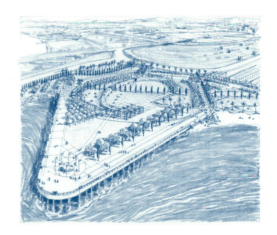

Artist's rendering of the proposed Point Arnold promenade at Middle Harbor Shoreline Park.

APPENDIX A1. PORT OF OAKLAND LOCATION MAP

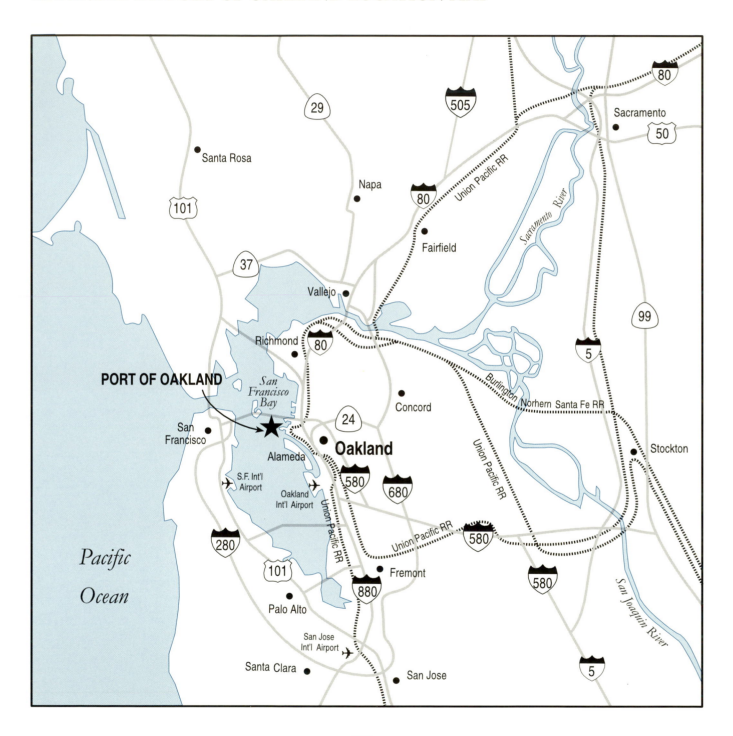

APPENDIX A2. FACILITIES OF THE PORT OF OAKLAND

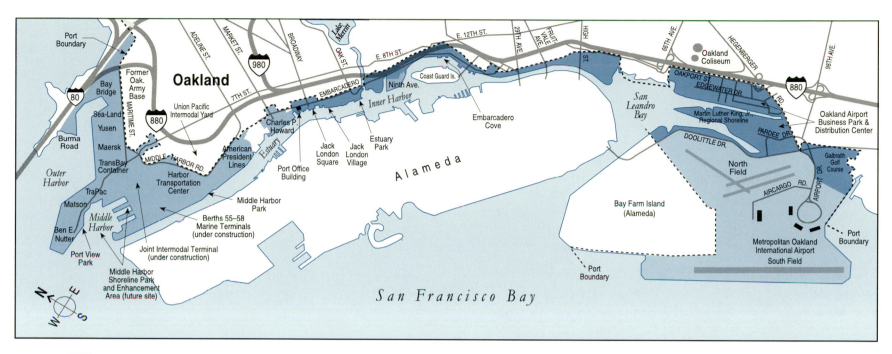

Aviation Division Area

Commercial Real Estate Division Area

Maritime Division Area

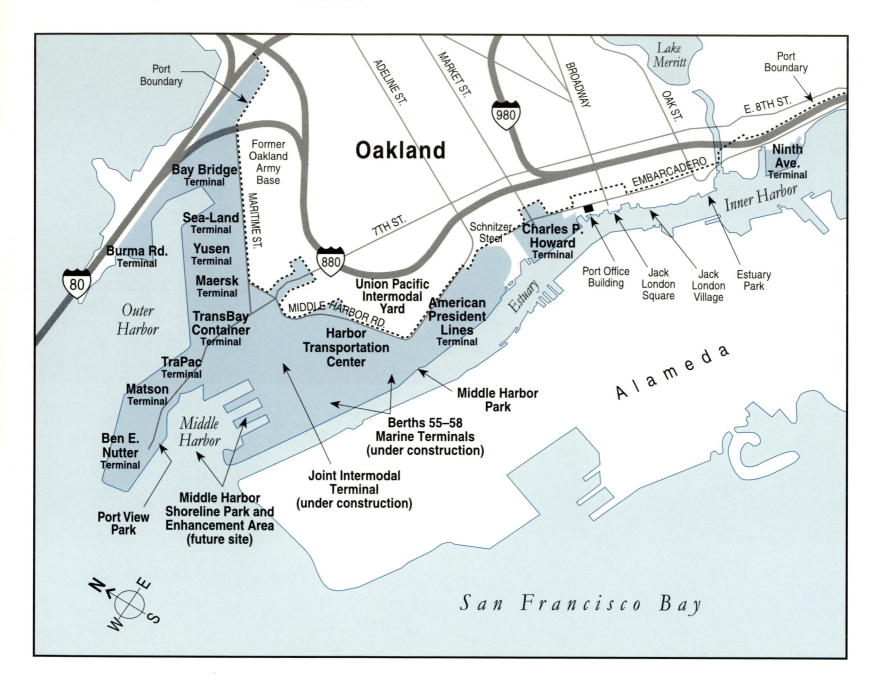

Port Boundary

Port Boundary

Lake Merritt

ADELINE ST.

MARKET ST.

BROADWAY

OAK ST.

980

E. 8TH ST.

Oakland

Former Oakland Army Base

Bay Bridge Terminal

MARITIME ST.

Ninth Ave. Terminal

Sea-Land Terminal

EMBARCADERO

Burma Rd. Terminal

Yusen Terminal

7TH ST.

880

Inner Harbor

80

Maersk Terminal

Schnitzer Steel

Charles P. Howard Terminal

TransBay Container Terminal

MIDDLE HARBOR RD.

Union Pacific Intermodal Yard

Estuary

Port Office Building

Jack London Square

Jack London Village

Estuary Park

Outer Harbor

TraPac Terminal

Harbor Transportation Center

American President Lines Terminal

Matson Terminal

A l a m e d a

Ben E. Nutter Terminal

Middle Harbor

Middle Harbor Park

Berths 55–58 Marine Terminals (under construction)

Middle Harbor Shoreline Park and Enhancement Area (future site)

Joint Intermodal Terminal (under construction)

Port View Park

N E S W

S a n   F r a n c i s c o   B a y

APPENDIX A4. AVIATION FACILITIES

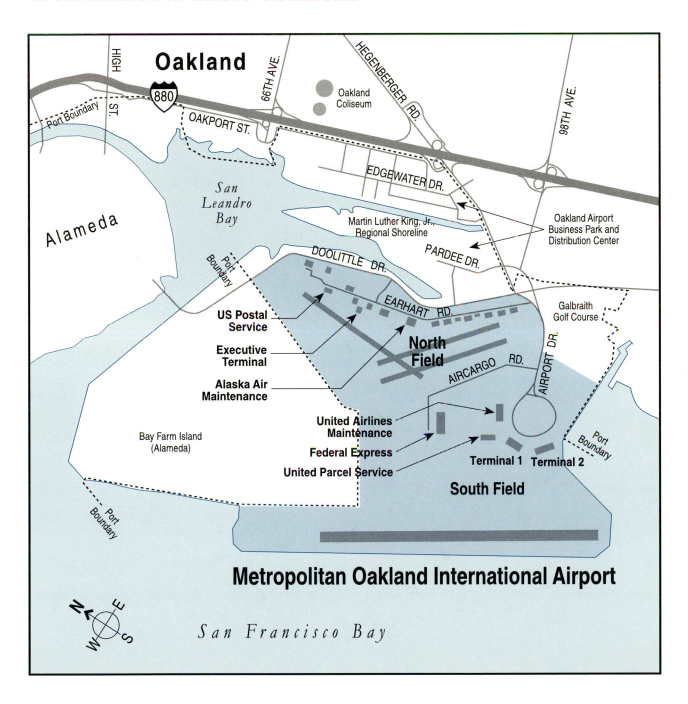

Oakland

880

HIGH ST.

66TH AVE.

HEGENBERGER RD.

98TH AVE.

Port Boundary

OAKPORT ST.

Oakland Coliseum

EDGEWATER DR.

San Leandro Bay

Alameda

Martin Luther King, Jr., Regional Shoreline

PARDEE DR.

Oakland Airport Business Park and Distribution Center

DOOLITTLE DR.

Port Boundary

EARHART RD.

Galbraith Golf Course

US Postal Service

North Field

Executive Terminal

AIRCARGO RD.

AIRPORT DR.

Alaska Air Maintenance

Bay Farm Island (Alameda)

United Airlines Maintenance

Port Boundary

Federal Express

United Parcel Service

Terminal 1   Terminal 2

Port Boundary

South Field

Metropolitan Oakland International Airport

N E W S

San Francisco Bay

APPENDIX A5. COMMERCIAL REAL ESTATE

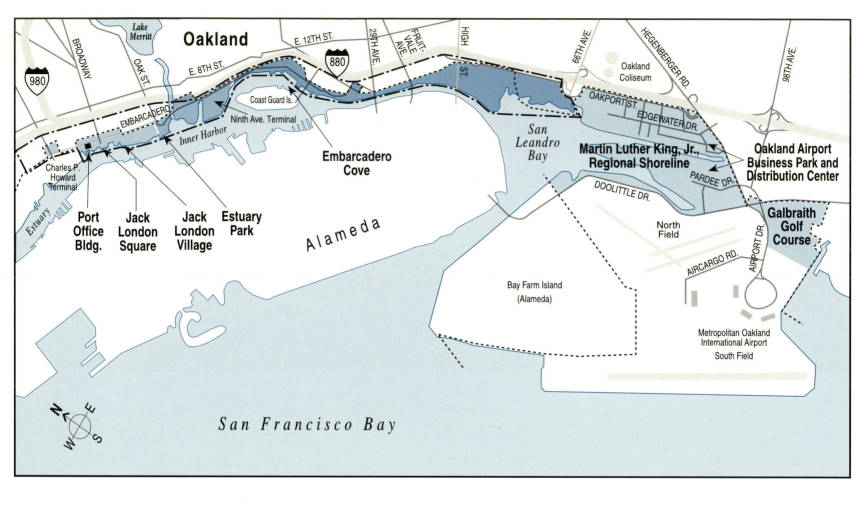

◼ COMMERCIAL REAL ESTATE

ESTUARY POLICY PLAN AREA
☐ Jack London District

☐ Oak-to-Ninth Avenue District

☐ San Antonio/Fruitvale District

- - - - - Port Area Line

— ∙ — ∙ — Estuary Policy Plan Area

NOTE: As of January 2000, the Port and the city are in discussions regarding a potential change in the Port Area Line affecting the Commercial Real Estate Area within the Estuary Policy Plan Area. Under this change, Port-owned property would remain in Port ownership, but the entire affected area would be regulated under city jurisdiction.

APPENDIX A6. OAKLAND 1859

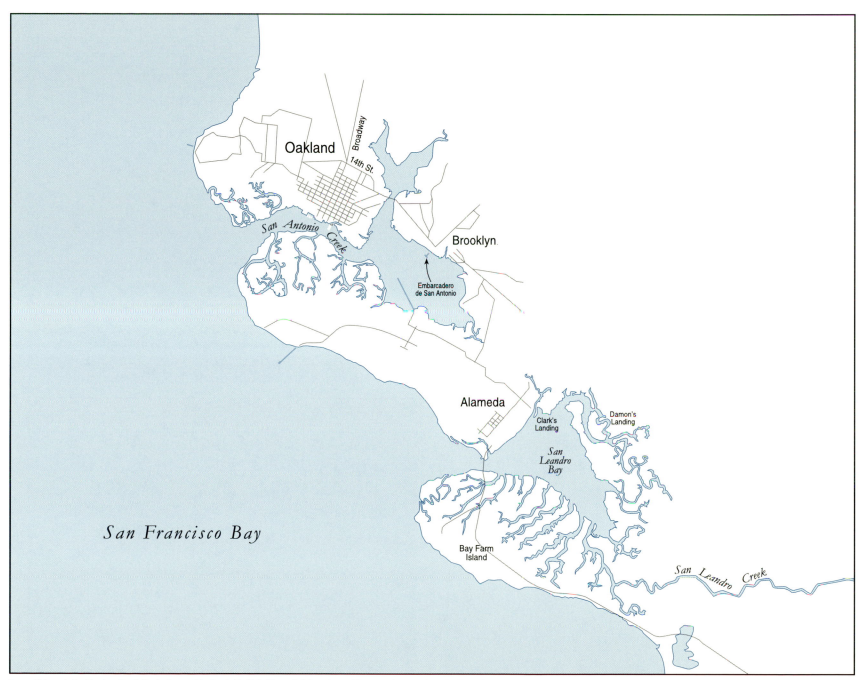

Source: Entrance to San Francisco Bay, California: Survey of the Coast of the United States, U.S. Coast Survey Office, 1859. Courtesy of the Map Room, Doe Library, University of California, Berkeley.

APPENDIX A7. OAKLAND 1906

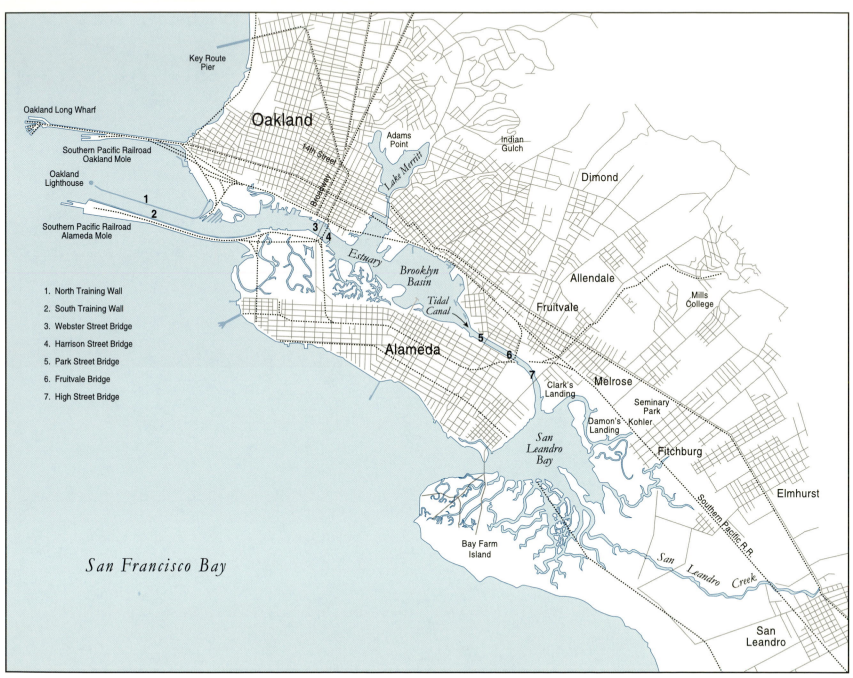

Key Route Pier

Oakland Long Wharf

Southern Pacific Railroad Oakland Mole

Oakland Lighthouse

Southern Pacific Railroad Alameda Mole

1. North Training Wall

2. South Training Wall

3. Webster Street Bridge

4. Harrison Street Bridge

5. Park Street Bridge

6. Fruitvale Bridge

7. High Street Bridge

Oakland

Adams Point

Indian Gulch

Dimond

14th Street

Broadway

Lake Merritt

Estuary

Brooklyn Basin

Tidal Canal

Allendale

Fruitvale

Mills College

Alameda

Clark's Landing

Melrose

Seminary Park

Damon's Landing

Kohler

Fitchburg

Elmhurst

San Leandro Bay

Bay Farm Island

San Francisco Bay

Southern Pacific R.R.

San Leandro Creek

San Leandro

Source: San Francisco Bay, Southern Part: West Coast, California, U.S. Coast & Geodetic Survey, 1906. Courtesy of the Map Room, Doe Library, University of California, Berkeley.

APPENDIX A8. OAKLAND 1925

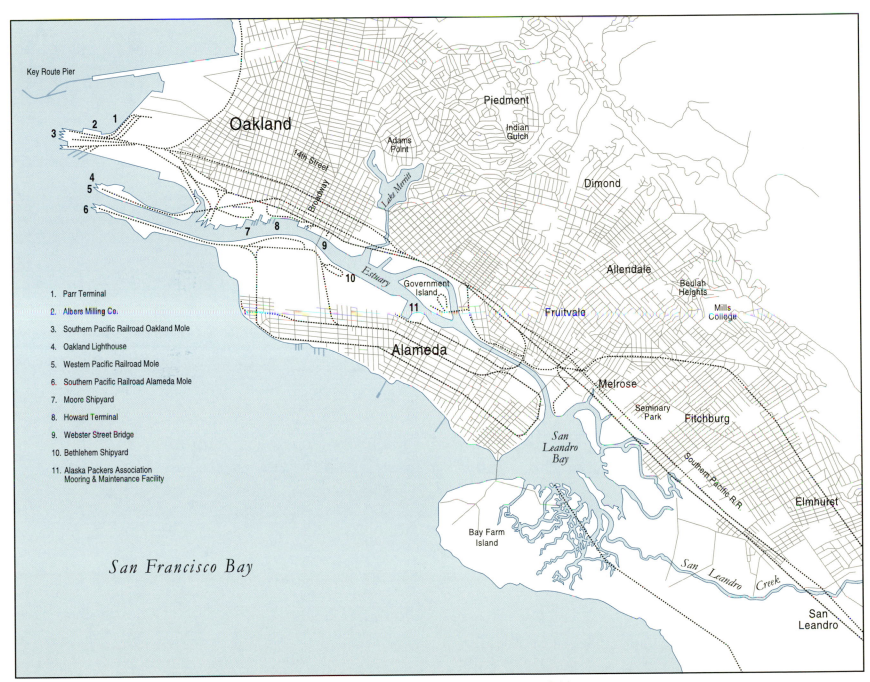

Key Route Pier

Oakland

Piedmont

Indian Gulch

Adams Point

14th Street

Broadway

Lake Merritt

Dimond

Estuary

Government Island

Allendale

Beulah Heights

Fruitvale

Mills College

1. Parr Terminal
2. Albers Milling Co.
3. Southern Pacific Railroad Oakland Mole
4. Oakland Lighthouse
5. Western Pacific Railroad Mole
6. Southern Pacific Railroad Alameda Mole
7. Moore Shipyard
8. Howard Terminal
9. Webster Street Bridge
10. Bethlehem Shipyard
11. Alaska Packers Association Mooring & Maintenance Facility

Alameda

Melrose

Seminary Park

Fitchburg

San Leandro Bay

Southern Pacific R.R.

Elmhurst

Bay Farm Island

San Leandro Creek

San Leandro

San Francisco Bay

Source: San Francisco Bay, Southern Part: West Coast, California, U.S. Coast & Geodetic Survey, 1925. Courtesy of the Map Room, Doe Library, University of California, Berkeley.

APPENDIX A9. OAKLAND 1949

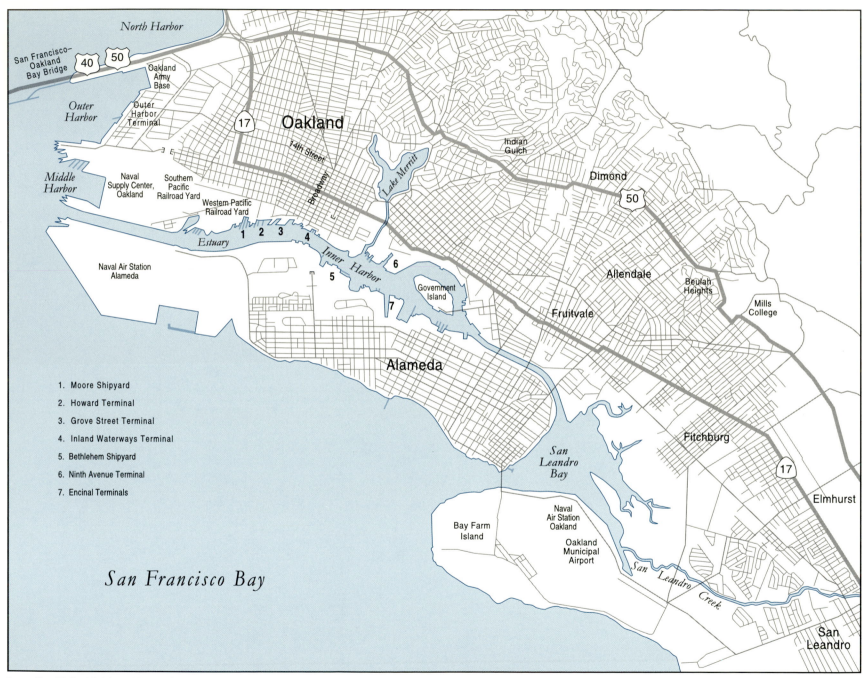

North Harbor

San Francisco-
Oakland
Bay Bridge

40 50

Oakland
Army
Base

Outer
Harbor

Outer
Harbor
Terminal

17 Oakland

Indian
Gulch

Lake Merritt

Dimond

50

Middle
Harbor

Naval
Supply Center,
Oakland

Southern
Pacific
Railroad Yard

Western Pacific
Railroad Yard

14th Street

Broadway

1 2 3 4

Estuary

Inner Harbor

6

Allendale

Beulah
Heights

Mills
College

Naval Air Station
Alameda

5

7

Government
Island

Fruitvale

Alameda

1. Moore Shipyard

2. Howard Terminal

3. Grove Street Terminal

4. Inland Waterways Terminal

5. Bethlehem Shipyard

6. Ninth Avenue Terminal

7. Encinal Terminals

San
Leandro
Bay

Fitchburg

17

Elmhurst

Bay Farm
Island

Naval
Air Station
Oakland

Oakland
Municipal
Airport

San Leandro Creek

San Francisco Bay

San
Leandro

Source: Map of Oakland, Berkeley and Alameda: California State Automobile Association, 1949. Courtesy of the Map Room, Doe Library, University of California, Berkeley.

APPENDIX B. OPERATING REVENUES OF THE PORT OF OAKLAND, 1928–1999

Sources: *Oakland City Auditor's Report* (1928–1967) and *Port of Oakland Annual Report* (1968–1998).

1928	$269,000	1943	$2,097,000	1958	$3,641,000	1973	$15,224,000	1988	$71,074,000
1929	$485,000	1944	$1,480,000	1959	$3,254,000	1974	$17,954,000	1989	$73,406,000
1930	$577,000	1945	$1,748,000	1960	$3,343,000	1975	$20,274,000	1990	$88,534,000
1931	$604,000	1946	$1,702,000	1961	$3,080,000	1976	$20,766,000	1991	$97,526,000
1932	$652,000	1947	$1,754,000	1962	$3,152,000	1977	$23,735,000	1992	$106,613,000
1933	$572,000	1948	$1,921,000	1963	$3,490,000	1978	$30,877,000	1993	$117,042,000
1934	$562,000	1949	$2,182,000	1964	$3,901,000	1979	$36,119,000	1994	$118,859,000
1935	$645,000	1950	$2,152,000	1965	$4,152,000	1980	$40,953,000	1995	$137,786,000
1936	$749,000	1951	$2,573,000	1966	$5,124,000	1981	$42,146,000	1996	$147,164,000
1937	$738,000	1952	$4,227,000	1967	$6,312,000	1982	$45,986,000	1997	$149,918,000
1938	$890,000	1953	$3,642,000	1968	$7,264,000	1983	$47,583,000	1998	$157,838,000
1939	$927,000	1954	$3,474,000	1969	$9,210,000	1984	$50,591,000	1999	$162,903,000
1940	$941,000	1955	$3,119,000	1970	$10,732,000	1985	$60,117,000		
1941	$940,000	1956	$3,151,000	1971	$11,248,000	1986	$67,219,000		
1942	$1,181,000	1957	$3,945,000	1972	$14,223,000	1987	$67,767,000		

Note: Year indicates fiscal year, ending June 30. Figures are rounded to nearest thousand.

APPENDIX C. OAKLAND BOARD OF PORT COMMISSIONERS, 1925–2000

The governing body of the Port of Oakland is the Oakland Board of Port Commissioners, whose members are appointed by the mayor with the approval of the Oakland City Council. A temporary board was formed on December 11, 1925. Following passage of a city-charter amendment in 1926, the first permanent board was appointed on January 20, 1927, and officially sworn in on February 12, 1927. The board originally had five members who served six-year terms. A 1968 charter amendment expanded the board to seven members and reduced the terms to four years. Commissioners who have served ten or more years are indicated by an asterisk (*).

Stuart S. Hawley	1925–27		Carl H. Hansen	1957–63		R. Zachary Wasserman	1987–90
Roscoe D. Jones	1925–28		Peter M. Tripp*	1959–75		Thomas J. Sweeney	1987–91
H. C. Capwell	1925–29		Joseph W. Chaudet	1961–67		Carole Ward Allen	1987–93
Ben F. Pendleton	1925–33		George J. Vukasin	1961–68		Ronald W. Brady	1988–91
Robert A. Leet*	1925–37		Edward G. Brown	1963–69		James B. Lockhart	1989–97
George C. Pardee*	1927–41		Emmett Kilpatrick	1963–69		Celso D. Ortiz	1989–98
Ralph T. Fisher*	1928–39		Robert E. Mortensen*	1967–77		Lionel J. Wilson	1990–91
Sherwood Swan	1930–31		William Walters	1968–77		Henry Chang, Jr.	1990–92
Leroy R. Goodrich	1931–37		A. Anthony Bilotti	1969–70		Alan C. Furth	1991–93
James J. McElroy*	1933–46		H. Boyd Gainor*	1969–79		Allen E. Broussard	1991–96
Frank Colbourn	1937–39		Y. Charles Soda*	1969–80		David Kramer	1991–
Eugene W. Roland	1937–43		Thomas L. Berkley*	1969–81		John Loh	1992–
Edward J. Smith	1939–45		Ted Connolly*	1970–82		James A. Vohs	1993–96
Claire V. Goodwin*	1939–51		Harry R. Lange	1975–79		Ada C. Cole	1993–97
Stanley J. Smith	1941–47		Henry J. Rodriguez	1977–81		Robert L. Harris	1996–
Clifford D. Allen	1943–49		Norvel Smith	1977–85		Becky L. Taylor	1996–
John F. Hassler	1945–46		David Creque	1979–84		Frank Kiang	1998–
Stanley A. Burgraff	1946–51		Herbert Eng	1979–88		Kathy Neal	1998–
Dudley W. Frost	1946–52		Douglas J. Higgins*	1980–90		Peter Uribe	1998–
James F. Galliano*	1947–59		G. William Hunter	1981–89			
H. W. Estep*	1949–61		Patricia Pineda	1981–89			
Dunlap C. Clark	1951–57		H. Wayne Goodroe	1982–87			
John F. Tulloch*	1951–63		Seymour Bachman	1984–87			
Nat Levy	1952–61		Christine Scotlan	1985–87			

PRESIDENTS OF THE BOARD OF PORT COMMISSIONERS, 1925–2000

The president of the board is elected by vote of the commissioners.

Roscoe D. Jones	1925–28	Y. Charles Soda	1971–72/1977–78
Ralph T. Fisher	1928–37	H. Boyd Gainor	1972–73/1978–79
James J. McElroy	1937–45	Thomas L. Berkley	1973–74/1979–80
John F. Hassler	1945–46	Ted Connolly	1974–75/1980–81
Claire V. Goodwin	1946–51	Norvel Smith	1981–82
Dudley W. Frost	1951–52	Herbert Eng	1982–83
James F. Galliano	1952–53/1957–58	Patricia Pineda	1983–84
H. W. Estep	1953–55/1958–59	H. Wayne Goodroe	1984–85
John F. Tulloch	1955–56/1959–60	Douglas J. Higgins	1985–86/1988–89
Nat Levy	1956–57/1960–61	G. William Hunter	1986–88
Peter M. Tripp	1961–63/1968/1971	Ronald W. Brady	1989–90
George J. Vukasin	1964	Carole Ward Allen	1990–92
Edward G. Brown	1965	James B. Lockhart	1992–96
Joseph W. Chaudet	1966	Allen E. Broussard	1996
Emmett Kilpatrick	1967	Celso D. Ortiz	1996–98
Robert E. Mortensen	1969/1975–76	John Loh	1998–
William Walters	1970/1976–77		

PORT MANAGERS AND EXECUTIVE DIRECTORS, 1926–2000

The Board of Port Commissioners appoints the chief staffperson at the Port of Oakland. Originally known as the "Port Manager and Chief Engineer," the title of this position was changed to "Executive Director" in 1952.

Gustave B. Hegardt	1926–32	Walter A. Abernathy	1977–89
Arthur H. Abel	1932–52	Nolan R. Gimpel	1990–91
Dudley W. Frost	1952–62	Charles R. Roberts	1991–95
Ben E. Nutter	1962–77	Charles W. Foster	1995–

APPENDIX D. SHIPPING LINES AT THE PORT OF OAKLAND, JANUARY 2000

Shipping Lines	Africa	Asia	Australia New Zealand	Europe	Hawaii	Latin America	Middle East	South Pacific
American President Lines		■	■			■		■
Australia-New Zealand Direct Line			■					■
China Ocean Shipping Co. (COSCO)		■						
Cho Yang Line		■		■		■		
CMA-CGM America, Inc.		■		■				
CCNI					■			
d'Amico Line	■			■	■			
DSR-Senator Lines		■		■	■	■		
Evergreen America Corporation		■				■		
Fesco Australia North American Line			■				■	
Hanjin Shipping Co.		■						
Hapag-Lloyd (America), Inc.		■		■				
Hyundai Merchant Marine America		■	■	■		■		
Italia Line	■			■	■			
"K" Line America, Inc.		■						
Maersk Line	■	■	■	■	■	■		
Matson Navigation Co.					■			■
Mitsui O.S.K. Lines (America), Inc.		■				■		
Norasia Lines		■						
NYK Line (North America), Inc.		■		■		■		
Orient Overseas Container Line (OOCL)		■	■					
PM&O Line								■
P&O Nedlloyd		■	■	■	■	■		
Pan Ocean Shipping						■		
Polynesia Line Ltd.								■
Saga Forrest Carriers	■							
Sea-Land Service		■	■	■	■	■		■
Star Shipping, Inc.				■				
Toko Line		■						
Toyofuji Shipping Co., Ltd.		■						
Yang Ming Line		■	■					
Zim Container Service		■		■	■			

SOURCES

General Sources

Official records and publications of the Port of Oakland contain a wealth of information about operations, activities, and facilities. Brochures and pamphlets have been produced with some regularity since the late 1920s. Illustrated magazines and newsletters (published on a more-or-less monthly basis) include the *Port of Oakland Compass* (1932–42); *Port of Oakland: Progress–News–Notes* (1959–72); *Progress: News and Events from the Port of Oakland* (1972–74); *Port Progress* (1974–95); and *Compass* (1996–present). Unillustrated progress reports were also issued on a monthly basis from as early as 1951 through 1959. Blueprints, land-acquisition maps, master plans, environmental documents, and the minutes of the Board of Port Commissioners were also consulted. *The Port of Oakland . . . Sixty Years: A Chronicle of Progress*, an illustrated chronology published in 1987 by the Port of Oakland Public Affairs Department, is a helpful introduction to the Port's history.

A number of books provided general information about local and regional history, including DeWitt Jones, ed., *History of the Port of Oakland, 1850–1934* (Oakland, 1934); Edgar J. Hinkel and William E. McCann, eds., *Oakland 1852–1938* (Oakland, 1939); Mel Scott, *The San Francisco Bay Area: A Metropolis in Perspective* (Berkeley and Los Angeles, 1959); David Weber, *Oakland: Hub of the West* (Tulsa, 1981); Beth Bagwell, *Oakland: The Story of a City* (Novato, California, 1982); and Charles Wollenberg, *Golden Gate Metropolis: Perspectives on Bay Area History* (Berkeley, 1985). The *Oakland Tribune Year Book*, published on a near-annual basis between 1911 and 1949, includes overviews of the Port of Oakland and earlier waterfront developments.

Maritime (Chapter 1 through Chapter 4)

John Haskell Kemble's *San Francisco Bay: A Pictorial Maritime History* (New York, 1957) remains one of the best general introductions to the region's rich maritime traditions. Joseph Jeremiah Hagwood, Jr., *Engineers at the Golden Gate: A History of the San Francisco District, U.S. Army Corps of Engineers, 1866–1980* (San Francisco, 1980) covers a wide range of harbor improvements and port developments on San Francisco Bay. Leslie A. Bryan, *Principles of Water Transportation* (New York, 1939); and A. G. Ford, *Handling and Stowage of Cargo* (Scranton, Pennsylvania, 1942) elucidate traditional methods of shipping and break-bulk cargo handling. Woodruff C. Minor, *On the Bay: A Centennial History of the Encinal Yacht Club* (Alameda, California, 1994) includes sections on local maritime history.

Detailed overviews of harbor improvements and shipping activity in Oakland since the 1870s are provided by the *Annual Report of the U.S. Engineer* (Washington, D.C., 1874–present). Sanborn-Perris insurance maps published between 1889 and 1952 depict the development of Oakland's waterfront. Werner Hegemann, "Report on a City Plan for the Municipalities of Oakland & Berkeley" (Oakland, 1915) includes a discussion of shipping and railroads. Gustave B. Hegardt, Charles D. Marx, and Charles T. Leeds, "Report on Port of Oakland" (Oakland, 1925) analyzes Oakland's strengths and weaknesses as a seaport and contains proposals for development.

Two indispensable sources for the history and practice of containerized shipping are Captain Warren H. Hastings, *Modern Marine Terminal Operations and Management* (Oakland, 1983), a textbook produced in cooperation with the Port of Oakland's Maritime Division (Raymond A. Boyle, ed.); and David R. McKenzie, Mark C. North, and Daniel S. Smith, *Intermodal Transportation—The Whole Story* (Omaha, Nebraska, 1989).

Aviation (Chapter 5 through Chapter 7)

Several standard histories were consulted for general themes, including Charles H. Gibbs-Smith, *Aviation: An Historical Survey from its Origins to the End of World War II* (London, 1970); and R. E. G. Davies, *Airlines of the United States Since 1914* (London, 1972). Early aviation in California is covered in part by Kenneth M. Johnson, *Aerial California: An Account of Early Flight in Northern & Southern California, 1849 to World War I* (Los Angeles, 1961); and William A. Schoneberger and Paul Sonnenburg, *California Wings: A History of Aviation in the Golden State* (Woodland Hills, California, 1984).

A good overview of the career of Weldon B. Cooke is contained in the October 1933 issue of the *Port of Oakland Compass*. Arue Szura, *Folded Wings: A History of Transocean Air Lines* (Missoula, Montana, 1989) is a lively account by a former employee. William Flynn, *Men, Money and Mud* (San Francisco, 1954) provides a short history of San Francisco Airport. Much of the early history of aviation in the East Bay has been pieced together from old newspaper articles; the reader is referred to "Air Alameda," Woodruff Minor's twenty-six-part series in the *Alameda Journal* newspaper (October 1994–May 1995) for a more detailed account.

The development of Oakland Municipal Airport is covered in the annual resumes of the *Oakland Tribune Year Book*; the annual airport issues of the *Port of Oakland Compass*; and various brochures and pamphlets issued by the Port of Oakland. The airport's later expansion is also amply documented in Port publications.

The Waterfront and the Community (Chapter 8 and Chapter 9)

Port of Oakland magazines, brochures, and progress reports were the primary sources of information for real-estate activities. The minutes of the Board of Port Commissioners elucidate the early development of Jack London Square and the Oakland Airport Business Park. Port publications were also the main sources for community and environmental issues. Several Environmental Impact Reports produced by the Port of Oakland help to clarify recent projects. Celia McCarthy, "A Management Plan for Maritime Cultural Resources Within the Jurisdiction of the Port of Oakland" (Master's thesis, Sonoma State University, 1999) provides an overview of historic preservation issues on the Oakland waterfront.

Pictorial Sources

Most of the images reproduced in this book are from the Port of Oakland's extensive archives of historic photographs. Other images were obtained from the Oakland History Room, Oakland Public Library; the Oakland Museum of California; the Bancroft Library and the Doe Library Map Room, University of California, Berkeley; the J. Porter Shaw Library, San Francisco Maritime National Historic Park; the Alameda Historical Museum; the Emeryville Historical Society; the Pat Hathaway Collection, Monterey; the East Bay Regional Park District; and Pacific Aerial Surveys, Oakland. Uncredited photographs are from the Port of Oakland Archives, which include thousands of pictures taken by many different commercial photographers.

Other uncredited images were reproduced from the following works: **2 upper left,** Stephen Powers, *Tribes of California,* University of California Press, 1976 (reprint of 1877 ed., Govt. Printing Office, Washington, issued as v. 3 of *Contributions to North American Ethnology*); **3 upper right,** Pearl Randolph Fibel, *The Peraltas,* Peralta Hospital, 1971; **3 center right,** *World Book Encyclopedia,* Vol. 8 ("G"), World Book-Childcraft International, Subsidiary of Field Enterprises, 1978; **7 lower right,** Robert S. Ford, *Red Trains in the East Bay,* Interurbans Publications, 1977; **69 lower right,** *San Francisco Chronicle,* February 3, 1912, p. 5; **75 lower right,** Leroy Abrams, *Illustrated Flora of the Pacific States,* Stanford University Press, 1940; **162 lower left,** Christopher M. Perrins, with International Council for Bird Preservation, *The Illustrated Encyclopedia of Birds,* Prentice Hall Press, 1990; **163 lower right,** Herbert Mason, *A Flora of the Marshes of California,* University of California Press, 1957.

INDEX